OPPORTUNITY AND DISADVANTAGE AT AGE 16

Policy Studies Institute (PSI) is one of Europe's leading independent research organisations undertaking studies of economic, industrial and social policy, and the workings of political institutions.

PSI is a registered charity, run on a non-profit basis, and is not associated with any political party, pressure group or commercial interest.

PSI attaches great importance to covering a wide range of subject areas with its multidisciplinary approach. The Institute's researchers are organised in groups which currently cover the following programmes:

Crime, Justice and Youth Studies – Employment – Ethnic Equality and Diversity – European Industrial Development – Family Finances – Information and Citizenship – Information and Cultural Studies – Social Care and Health Studies – Work, Benefits and Social Participation

This publication arises from the Crime, Justice and Youth Studies programme and is one of over 30 publications made available by the Institute each year.

Information about the work of PSI and a catalogue of available books can be obtained from:

External Relations Department, PSI
100 Park Village East, London NW1 3SR

Opportunity and Disadvantage at Age 16

Ann Hagell and Catherine Shaw

POLICY STUDIES INSTITUTE
London

PSI
PUBLISHING

The publishing imprint of the independent
POLICY STUDIES INSTITUTE
100 Park Village East, London NW1 3SR
Tel. 0171 468 0468   Fax. 0171 388 0914

ISBN 0 85374 680 X
PSI Report 814

PSI publications are available from:
BEBC Distribution Ltd.
P O Box 1496, Poole, Dorset, BH12 3YD

Books will normally be dispatched within 24 hours. Cheques should be made
payable to BEBC Distribution Ltd.

Credit cards and telephone/fax orders may be placed on the following
freephone numbers:
FREEPHONE 0800 262260
FREEFAX   0800 262266

Book trade Representation (UK & Eire):
Broadcast Books
24 Dr Montfort Road, London SW16 1LZ
Tel. 0181 677 5129

PSI subscriptions are available from PSI's subscription agent
Carfax Publishing Company Ltd.
P O Box 25, Abingdon, Oxford OX14 3UE

Printed in Great Britain by Redwood Books, Trowbridge, Wiltshire

Contents

Tables and figures

Tables

Figures

Preface and acknowledgements

As we approach the close of this century, the spotlight on young people and their role and place in society is becoming increasingly intense. The last 25 years have witnessed enormous changes in the experiences of 16 and 17 year olds as the youth labour market has shrunk and the numbers staying on in education have rocketed. Public concern over both the vulnerability of children and, in parallel (and in contradiction), increases in youth crime, have promoted the perception of a crisis in the future of young people. In the mid-1990s, newspaper headlines proclaiming a growing underclass of alienated young people are not unusual.

At the centre of the concern over young people is a focus on particularly disadvantaged groups; those growing up in the inner cities, those from ethnic minorities, those who do not achieve good examination results. The study reported in this book was designed specifically to address the experiences of such young people as they reached the end of their compulsory schooling.

The study, called *Changing Lives,* involved a major survey of over 3,000 inner city 16 year olds from 34 schools within six urban areas of England. The young people surveyed in this study became eligible to leave school in spring or summer of 1993, and questionnaires were mailed out at three points during the 1993/94 academic year. The research design allowed a thorough examination of initial post-school destinations. In addition, it provided information on progress, satisfaction and further transitions (for example, college drop-outs and trainees moving into employment), as well as comparing the differential experiences of young women and men and members of different ethnic minorities.

Preliminary results from each of the three waves of data collection have been presented in brief reports by Catherine Shaw, issued by the Policy Studies Institute in 1994. This book summarises and draws together the earlier results, and presents new and in-depth analyses integrating all three waves. In so doing, it presents an overview of the whole project, and supersedes the preliminary reports.

Changing Lives was funded by a consortium of research sponsors, including: Barclays Bank PLC, Birmingham Training and Enterprise Council (TEC), British Telecommunications PLC, the Commission for

Company Ltd, Kingfisher PLC, Leeds TEC, Lloyds Bank Charitable Trust PLC, London East TEC, Manchester TEC, Marks and Spencer PLC, Merseyside TEC, The Pilgrim Trust, Shell UK Ltd, South Thames TEC and United Biscuits (UK) Ltd. We are very grateful to them for their support, in particular to Clyde Williams who chaired the project's advisory group. Thanks are due to the 34 schools who took part and helped to administer the survey and we are, of course, indebted to the many young people who took the time and effort to complete the questionnaires.

Many people at the Policy Studies Institute have been involved in *Changing Lives* over the last two years, and we would particularly like to acknowledge the role of David J Smith and Jane Lakey who initiated the project, and Dr Tim Newburn who took over the project's management on David's departure to the University of Edinburgh.

Pathways and choices at age 16

Changing Lives: **Introduction and aims**

A number of political and social changes over the last 25 years have meant that the experiences of young people on leaving compulsory education have changed dramatically. Far fewer young people now go into work at this point in their lives, and many more are involved in continuing education instead. In addition, in 1988, benefits were withdrawn from virtually all unemployed 16-18 year olds. New vocational qualifications have been developed, and a series of government sponsored training initiatives has been introduced, beginning with the Youth Opportunities Programme and developing into the current provision of Youth Training (YT) and Youth Credits.

Against this background, several general concerns underpinned the development of the *Changing Lives* project. First, it is widely recognised across the political spectrum that there is a need for the workforce to be better educated, more adaptable, more highly skilled, and better trained (see, for example, the National Commission on Education, 1993). Second, it is also widely recognised that the British educational system is very effective for high achievers from middle class homes, but that the standards achieved by the majority of pupils are much poorer than they should be (Smith and Noble, 1995). The relatively poor performance of pupils attending schools in inner urban areas has been highlighted by the publication of 'league tables' of academic attainment; every one of the bottom 30 local education authorities in the GCSE league tables in 1992 was in an urban area, some of which suffered 'substantial deprivation' (Barber, 1993). Arising from this, there is a need to reduce inequalities of opportunity; between less and more affluent areas, between social classes, and between ethnic groups (eg. Wilkinson, 1994).

Changing Lives was set in the context of existing national findings about youth from major longitudinal projects such as the Youth Cohort Survey funded by the Department for Education and Employment, and the research funded by the Economic and Social Research Council as part of its '16-19 Initiative'. In order to produce complementary data about more disadvantaged groups, the *Changing Lives* study aimed to focus on young people in major cities, exploring the critical transition from compulsory education and showing to what extent adolescents from different groups take advantage of training and educational opportunities in the early 1990s. How well were training and educational programmes adapted to their needs? How did the experiences of young people from the main ethnic minority groups differ? We concentrated on a number of urban areas of social and economic stress, where substantial proportions of the population belonged to ethnic minority groups. This did not provide, of course, a nationally representative sample, but one specifically selected to reflect our interests.

PSI has a long history of interest in youth, in restricted opportunity, and in the labour market. *Changing Lives* was an opportunity to bring some of these interests together. A series of PSI studies of ethnic minorities has suggested that structural inequalities contribute to restricted access to higher education (Modood and Shiner, 1994, Shiner and Newburn, 1995), and to promotions (Beishon, Virdee and Hagell, 1995), and have emphasised the importance of considering ethnic diversity rather than homogeneity (Modood, Beishon and Virdee, 1995, Jones, 1993). Our work on young offenders located their behaviour and experiences within the framework of disadvantaged and disrupted social worlds (Hagell and Newburn, 1994), while PSI analysis of the Youth Cohort Study clarified some of the routes beyond compulsory education for a nationally representative cohort of young people (Payne, 1995a and 1995b). With *Changing Lives* we sought to fill a gap, but ideally would consider the survey as a start rather than a conclusion.

The *Changing Lives* study, described in detail in the chapters that follow, consisted of a survey of over 3,000 young people whose names appeared on the 1992/93 Year 11 registers of 34 secondary schools located in six inner city areas. Questionnaires were completed by members of the sample at three points during the first year following compeletion of their compulsory schooling.

As a background, the remainder of this chapter explores existing data relating to the education and labour market experiences of young people leaving compulsory education in the United Kingdom (UK).

Chapters 2 and 3 describe the methodology and sampling of the *Changing Lives* study in more detail. In Chapter 4, the respondents' academic and vocational qualifications are described, together with their attitudes to school and beliefs about education, reasons for absence from school, and the usefulness of careers advice received. Their initial destinations at age 16 are outlined in Chapter 5. Chapter 6 uses the month by month accounts of what respondents did in the year covered by the project, breaking these up into distinct pathways taken, such as into full-time further education, or directly into the labour market. Multivariate analyses were used to predict the routes followed by various sub-groups within the sample, and the results of these analyses are reported in Chapter 7. Two chapters (8 and 9) look in more detail at respondents' reports of their experiences over the year, and the problems they faced. The final chapter (10) summarises the findings and draws some policy conclusions.

Education and labour market experiences beyond compulsory education

Recent years have seen the publication of a series of influential reports about the changes in the experiences of young people over the last few decades, including those by Rutter and Smith (1995), Wilkinson (1994) and Banks et al (1992). One of the main issues under discussion has been a move towards Continental patterns of extended transition to the labour market. Alongside postponement of employment has come an increase in training and staying-on rates. Contributing factors in this situation have included the advent of the single European market in 1992, upheavals in the UK labour market, the recession of the late 1980s, and changes in the UK benefit systems. In support of his seminal definition of adolescence as a period of identity confusion, Erik Erikson (1968) quoted Biff in Arthur Miller's *Death of a Salesman*: 'I just can't take hold, Mom, I can't take hold of some kind of a life'. A respondent to the *Changing Lives* surveys suggested that, at the moment, the problem was not so much one of taking hold but one of breaking loose. His analysis was that young people needed to 'feel free from being sort of tied up'.

What 'ties up' adolescents? In terms of the transition from full-time education to the labour market, choices at the end of compulsory education could be said to be increasingly limited. It is true that this century has seen a prolongation of education, accompanied by a parallel

3

increase in scholastic achievements, due at least in part to the opening up of educational opportunities to a much larger proportion of the population. However, in the early 1980s, youth unemployment in the UK rose to approximately one in four (of the 16-24 age group). The most recent increases in the numbers staying on in education need to be seen partly as a response to the lack of other opportunities. Unemployment in this age group has now fallen dramatically, as it has in other parts of Europe, but this is largely due to increases in programmes of training rather than any improvement in the youth labour market. On the contrary, it is becoming less and less likely that young people will find jobs in their late teens. Even unemployment ceased to be economically viable for school-leavers in 1988 when benefits for the 16-18 age group were substantially reduced. Since that date, 16 and 17 year olds can no longer be officially unemployed, and only in exceptional circumstances can young people of this age claim benefit.

Essentially, participation in the labour market (either employed or unemployed) has been replaced by training or staying on at school. Although commentators are agreed that the pattern of adolescent transitions is changing, what is less clear is how these recent changes have differentially affected groups of young people. In particular, how are those who are already disadvantaged by their backgrounds and circumstances coping with life following the end of their compulsory education? How do those from the inner cities cope in a situation of increasingly restricted options? What is happening to those from different ethnic minority groups as they move on at this stage?

There are two sides to most critical transitions. On one side is a structure of opportunities and constraints embodied for example in schools, higher education institutions and labour markets. On the other side are personal expectations and aspirations, which are likely to be partly determined by the immediate family and social context. What happens to young people is the result of an interaction between the opportunities and constraints surrounding them on one hand, and their own aspirations and concrete efforts on the other.

In England and Wales, the end of compulsory education comes at Easter of Year 11 for those who turn 16 by January, and in the summer for those with birthdays falling after January. There are four main routes for teenagers coming to the end of their compulsory education: to continue in education for at least another year, to embark on a vocational training course, to attempt to enter the labour market directly as an employee, or to do none of these things (caring for relatives, or travelling for example). In practice, distinctions between these routes are not always clear, particularly in the areas of employment and training, where employer-based YT, apprenticeships and employment with training may all have very similar features. In addition, the routes are not necessarily exclusive and may be combined, given expanding opportunities for part-time work and study. Nevertheless, the vast majority of 16 year olds will embark on one or other of the four outline paths described.

For young people as a whole, much of the recent evidence concerning what they actually do and the nature of these transitions comes from the British national longitudinal studies or from the Economic and Social Research Council (ESRC) 16-19 Initiative. The main features of these projects are outlined in Table 1.1. The longitudinal studies are a rich source of data, particularly the National Child Development Study (NCDS, eg Kerckhoff, 1990) and the Youth Cohort Study (YCS, eg Payne, 1995a, Courtenay and McAleese, 1993). The NCDS recruited virtually all children born in Scotland, Wales and England during one week in March 1958 (approximately 17,000) and has followed them into adulthood. The YCS is a series of studies of nationally representative young people (approximately 18,000 in the most recent sweep) designed to monitor their decisions and behaviour as they take up post-compulsory education or enter the labour force, again following them up at regular intervals. The ESRC's 16-19 Initiative (eg, Banks et al, 1992) was a programme of research on young people conducted by research teams in the Universities of Surrey, Sheffield, Liverpool, Dundee and Edinburgh. The aim of the initiative was to examine the political and economic socialisation of young people, including how they make their way into the economic and occupational structure, as well as finding out about their home lives, attitudes and politics. At the core of the programme was a longitudinal study of 5,000 young people growing up in four labour markets, in which two groups aged 15-16 and 17-18 were followed up for two years in the late 1980s. A separately funded element of the research compares the transitions made by the young people entering two of the British labour markets and those entering comparable labour markets in Germany (Bynner and Roberts, 1991).

Looking at the results from these studies highlights the fact that it is crucial to examine the transition from compulsory education to the labour market within the contemporary political and historical context. In the UK this has changed even in the relatively short period since the

Table 1.1   Major British longitudinal surveys of young people

Study	Sample
National Child Development Study (eg. Kerkoff, 1990)	17,000 people born in one week in March 1958, followed up at regular intervals into adulthood
ESRC 16-18 Initiative (eg. Banks et al, 1992; Evans and Heinz, 1994; Connolly et al, 1992)	Programme of research on young people in the 1980s, conducted by research teams at the Universities of Surrey, Sheffield, Liverpool, Dundee and Edinburgh, core study was of 5,000 young people in four labour markets, split into two groups (15-16 year olds and 17-18 year olds) followed for two years.
Youth Cohort Study (eg. Payne, 1995a & b; Drew et al, 1992)	Series of studies of nationally representative young people (18,000 in the most recent sweep) designed to monitor their progress into the labour market, funded by the DfEE

end of the ESRC 16-19 Initiative. Thus, referring to the transition from school to work made by the NCDS sample in the 1960s, Kerckhoff (1990) wrote that his comparison with US figures 'highlights the ways in which a society structures the transition process' (p83). However, although societal contexts have changed, there are valuable findings from the earlier projects which may still be relevant for schoolleavers today.

At the time that the NCDS sample left compulsory education in the 1970s, the majority of young Britons entered the labour force at 16 or 17. The majority of the NCDS cohort (98 per cent) had held a job by the age of 23 years, and 80 per cent had entered the labour force full-time before the age of 19. Less than one third had any full-time schooling past the age of 17, and less than one fifth had any past the age of 18.

Kerckhoff (1990) identified two main pathways taken by the NCDS cohort. The first was followed by those who remained in school longer, later moving directly from full-time education to full-time work. They rarely continued to study or get qualifications after starting work, and did little in the way of part-time further education. Those following the second pathway left school fairly early, and entered the labour force full-time. Many obtained additional qualifications through part-time further education while working. Those on the second path tended to be more disadvantaged but there were advantages in having this path open to them. Kerckhoff wrote:

> There was a clear early identification of those who did and did not have a chance to be successful within the regular school system ... Britons engaged in a tournament in which some won and were thus sponsored, but in which there was also a 'losers bracket'. Those who lost out in the first rounds in the regular school system had the opportunity to try again in the further education system. Those who failed to advance in the 'closed' system of regular education had a second chance in the more 'open' system of further education. (p189)

Kerckhoff (1990) identified three main factors affecting adolescent transitions at this age in the 1970s: individual characteristics, educational and labour force market conditions, and other events associated with moving into adulthood such as early childbirth. Kerckhoff emphasised the structural effects of different school types in determining the level of qualifications students took with them to the world of work, and he found that level of qualifications was the primary explanation of the prestige level of the first job that the cohort members obtained. Although the pathways taken were very different from those identified later in the 1980s in the 16-19 Initiative, the factors affecting the choice of pathway closely resembled those identified by Banks et al (1992) from the ESRC Initiative. However, it is worth noting the almost complete lack of reference to ethnicity in the NCDS report.

Looking at transitions made some 10 to 15 years later, Banks et al (1992) reported wide variations in the movement from full-time school to employment by the late 1980s. By this time, restrictions in employment opportunities for this age group were already quite severe, and only a minority moved straight from school to full-time employment at 16. The proportion doing so varied by area, from a maximum of 25 per cent to a minimum of 10 per cent in the areas studied. Among those who did not, there were two quite distinct groups. One passed through an intermediate stage of some form of training scheme (between 17 per cent and one third), and the other continued with a further period of full-time education either in school or at a college of some kind (between 40 and 60 per cent). Broadly speaking, the more advantaged members of the sample followed this latter route, and this was the best option in terms of future possibilities. The group who went straight into employment gained instant money and status, but did not necessarily do better in the long run. The group who passed into the 'training' phase were potentially the worst off. They tended to be those who lacked educational credentials and who were restricted by local labour force factors. If their training was not part of, or did not lead to, employment, then members of this group often drifted into peripheral unskilled employment interspersed with unemployment. Essentially, three crucial factors emerged in determining the pathway taken: educational achievement, local labour-market conditions and social background. Again, references to ethnicity are few, although much of the discussion centres around the effects of social class, family background, gender and various forms of inequality.

Three of the four main pathways open to today's 16 year olds that were outlined at the beginning of this section – education, training, work, or doing something else – involve prolonging the transition from education into the labour market (although, in fact, some YT training is technically 'employed status'). These three vary in terms of whether the delay is voluntary or involuntary, and Banks et al (1992) suggested that there was most room to exercise control if taking the education route. Those in the 16-18 Initiative studies who went into training in the 1980s seemed often to do so because there were no other options open to them. In addition, of the various routes open, the employment prospects looked best for those who were involved in vocational education, whereas they were worst for those on the YTS route.

A few years later, when the fourth, fifth and sixth YCS cohorts were under study (1989 to 1992) the rapid growth in the proportion of 16-17 year olds in full-time education was even more notable. In a YCS report on *Routes beyond compulsory schooling*, Payne (1995a) shows that 66 per cent of the sample completing compulsory education in 1992 stayed on in full-time education, and a further 15 per cent went into Youth Training. Only 11 per cent took a full-time job, and the remaining 8 per cent were doing none of these things, involved instead in part-time work, seeking work or training, or doing something else. Payne's analyses demonstrate that the staying-on rates increased most for those with the least qualifications. For the group with low or no GCSE passes, staying-on rates doubled in three years. At the time of writing, data are not yet available on Sweep 7 of the YCS, who left compulsory education in the same year as the *Changing Lives* cohort (in 1993). It is expected, however, that the increase in staying on has continued.

This brief account of previous findings concerning the period after finishing compulsory education highlights the importance of the particular political, economic and historical context in which the *Changing Lives* cohort were making their choices at 16. The early 1990s saw quite significantly changing circumstances in relation to post-16 activities. First, during the 1980s numbers of young people staying on in full-time education were for the first time greater than the numbers leaving and the trend is obviously continuing into the 1990s. Second, the introduction and growth of General National Vocational Qualifications and the increasing flexibility of academic and vocational education and training have complicated the situation. The choices facing young people at the end of their compulsory education have become increasingly complex with every year that passes.

The education and labour market options for 16 year olds in 1993

What were these choices for the *Changing Lives* cohort in the autumn of 1993? The contents page of the booklet *It's Your Choice,* published on behalf of the DfE, lists the main options in 1994, demonstrating the range and complexity of the options available. These options are presented in Table 1.2.

The main educational routes are broken down by the level of academic attainment achieved. For those with good results, further academic qualifications can be taken (A levels or more GCSEs). In addition, or instead, at all levels a choice to do vocational qualifications can be made, with the level of qualification taken depending on previous GCSE results. Thus, for example, for the better qualified, the vocational option includes Advanced and Intermediate levels of the GNVQ, whereas further down the scale the option is for Foundation GNVQs. NVQs are a possibility for all levels. Study could be continued at school, or at college. It could go on for one year, or for more. Those wanting to go to university would usually have to take the A Level pathway. It is also possible, of course, for those with lower GCSE results to take a relevant course with a view to then taking A levels and going on into higher education.

For those deciding to try and enter the labour market, full-time employment might be a possibility, as would youth training, or a job

Table 1.2   **Choices following the end of compulsory education, 1994 (adapted from the DfE booklet** *It's Your Choice***)**

Choices for people with good GCSEs (4 or more at grades A-C)
- choosing GCE A levels and Advanced Supplementary (AS) courses
- choosing an Advanced GNVQ
- choosing NVQs

Choices for people with some GCSEs
- choosing more GCSEs
- choosing an Intermediate GNVQ
- choosing NVQs

Choices for people with few or no GCSEs
- choosing more GCSEs
- choosing a Foundation GNVQ (or you may able to start at Intermediate level)
- choosing NVQs

Choices for people choosing a job with training
- choosing NVQs
- choosing Youth Training

Thinking about where to take a course
- choosing a school sixth form
- choosing a college

Some other choices
- choosing Youth Training
- thinking about work
- self-employment
- European choices

More ideas
- success ahead
- young people with disabilities
- money facts
- job hunting
- making applications
- being interviewed

GCSE	General Certificate of Secondary Education
A Levels	Advanced Level GCE
GNVQ	General National Vocational Qualification
NVQ	National Vocational Qualification

For further definitions of qualifications and training options, see the Glossary in Appendix 1.

that also offers NVQs. Self-employment or working in Europe are also mentioned.

For many young people, making a choice at the end of Year 11 involves more than simply weighing up career ambitions, local opportunities and qualifications gained. For those living in low-income families, the financial implications of each choice must be considered. Chatrik and Maclagan (1995) chart some of the obstacles and pitfalls which prevent young people making a smooth transition from school to the labour market. They point out that demand for discretionary further education awards from Local Education Authorities (LEAs) is increasing at a time when the amount available is decreasing in real terms, leading to smaller amounts being awarded and larger numbers of disappointed applicants. Whilst those opting for a YT place will at least have some income, this is decreasing in value year by year, the YT allowance for 16 year olds having been frozen at £29.50 since 1989 and that for 17 year olds remaining at £35 since 1986. Completing the picture of increasing hardship for young people, Chatrik and Maclagan quote *The New Earnings Survey 1993*, which reveals that in 1992/1993 wages for both young men and young women under the age of 18 were actually falling, at a time when wages for adult workers were rising.

This section has shown that there are important similarities and differences in the types of pathways followed by 16 year olds depending on historical context. At all times, some are 'losers' and some 'winners'; at all times the full-time educational pathway seems the most protective, at all times we see an interaction between the three factors of academic attainment, local labour market conditions and social background. The crucial focus of the *Changing Lives* survey was on those most likely to be taking the alternative, less protective pathways, or those most likely to be vulnerable to discrimination and restricted choices. The following sections look at what is known about the pathways of those from ethnic minorities, from the inner cities or from backgrounds indicating multiple disadvantage.

The role of ethnicity

Against the general picture of the pathways available to today's 16 year olds on leaving compulsory education, it must be borne in mind that different ethnic groups not only have different social and cultural backgrounds, but also have different patterns of educational attainment and opportunity, and thus their pathways are likely to vary. Evidence

11

from various studies over the last decade has suggested these differences are noticeable during their school years, at the point where they leave compulsory education, and in the years following school.

School attainment

The Swann Report (DES, 1985) examined the situation in six LEAs with high concentrations of ethnic minorities in 1978/79 and 1981/82. This found 'Asian leavers to be achieving very much on a par with, and in some cases marginally better than, their school fellows from all other groups in the same LEAs' (quoted in Smith and Tomlinson, 1989, p7) though, by contrast, African-Caribbeans were found to have poorer results than Asians and other peers. The 1980s saw the publication of several research projects addressing the issue. In a review of ethnic group differences in examination results, Drew and Gray (1991) report a fairly stable picture emerging. There is a good deal of consensus that African-Caribbean students perform less well than their Asian and white counterparts. There was usually little difference in the overall performance of Asian and white students. Looking at the distribution of examination results for the various samples in their review, Drew and Gray calculated that the gap between the white group and the African-Caribbeans was generally between one third and one half of a standard deviation. The gap was usually more pronounced at the bottom end of the distribution.

Although focus on ethnicity was noticeably absent from the earlier longitudinal studies described in the previous section, the YCS has been specifically analysed to track the progress of the ethnic minority group members in the sample. In a later report, Drew et al (1992) merged two early years of the YCS, giving a total sample of 28,000 nationally representative adolescents, and compared the education and labour-market experiences of different ethnic groups in the mid 1980s. There were approximately 900 Asian and nearly 500 African-Caribbean young people in their analyses. Once again, the African-Caribbean group achieved far fewer higher graded passes at GCSE (11 per cent) than the Asian students (24 per cent) or the white students (26 per cent).

Studies that have looked at progress throughout the secondary school years have concluded that, although their final level of attainment may vary, the various ethnic minority groups were *progressing* through secondary school at the same pace as their peers, given earlier levels of attainment (eg. Maughan and Rutter, 1986, Smith and Tomlinson, 1989). Such studies have also suggested that some ethnic minorities may do better in certain types of schools (Tomlinson, 1990). Further work is needed to untangle the ultimate causes of the differences in their attainment by age 16, and to look more closely at ethnic diversity in attainment. The important point to note is that some groups, most obviously African-Caribbean groups, start out on their chosen post-16 route already disadvantaged. Tomlinson (1990) has noted that the educational discrepancies between ethnic groups will become increasingly important in the urban technological societies of the 1990s.

Options and choices at age 16

Whether their achievements at 16 are in advance of or behind those of their white peers, several studies have concluded that young people from some ethnic minorities are more likely to continue their education. For example, Drew et al (1992) report very high levels of participation in further education by the students from ethnic minorities. Fifty-one per cent of the African-Caribbean group stayed on as did 67 per cent of the Asian group. Drew et al concluded that ethnic origin was in fact the most important factor in determining the chances of staying on, outweighing all other socio-economic characteristics. Even in the lower socio-economic groups, those from ethnic minorities were more likely to stay on. The reasons for this pattern are undoubtedly complex, Smith and Tomlinson (1989) suggesting that it may reflect not only a greater motivation towards self-improvement within ethnic minority communities but also an awareness of racial discrimination in the job market.

Drew et al describe much diversity in the paths taken once in post-compulsory education. However, there was a tendency for the African-Caribbean students to take more vocational courses than their white counterparts, and for the Asian students to retake GCSEs before transferring to A levels. The African-Caribbean group had done less well as a whole in their Year 11 examinations and so the vocational option may have made more sense for them.

This pattern of results has been fairly consistent over recent years. *The Swann Report* (DES, 1985) also provided information on the destinations of school leavers. In the five LEAs with high ethnic minority populations that participated in the second stage of the research, a higher proportion of South Asians and African-Caribbeans were staying on in full-time education – 33 per cent and 28 per cent respectively – than were other groups, who averaged 17 per cent at that time. Similarly, the 1982 PSI national survey of ethnic minorities found that in the 16-19 age range, twice as many South Asians as whites were staying on and, although young African-Caribbean men were no more likely to stay on, young African-Caribbean women were significantly more likely to do so (Brown, 1984).

Young people from ethnic minority groups demonstrate their greater commitment to further education in a variety of ways, beyond simple staying-on rates at 16. Drew et al also found that ethnic minority students remained in post-16 education for longer than white students. In later YCS analyses, Payne (1995a) concluded that students from ethnic minority groups were less likely than others to drop out of GCE A levels both overall and after controlling for GCSE results.

For those young people from ethnic minorities who elected not to stay on in education, preferring to take their chances in the labour market, the situation is less positive. There is evidence that, if they chose the training pathway, young people from ethnic minorities may be less likely to end up on those employer based schemes which offer most chance of skilled or higher status work. This was one conclusion drawn by Cross, Wrench and Barnett (1990), in their analysis of ethnic minorities and the Careers Service. One of the most worrying findings of their study was that this was partly attributable to the fact that careers officers were less likely to recommend the best training schemes to ethnic minorities. The authors go on to say,

> We have also found that ethnic minority school leavers are less likely to find work straight from school than are their white peers. In this context, the advice offered by a careers officer does not always seem to be the best for enhancing social mobility, and at worst could reflect judgements based on short-term criteria or stereotyped assumptions. (p81)

This was despite the fact that the aspirations of some ethnic minority groups were significantly higher than those of white students. The authors continue to draw even more damning conclusions:

> The evidence suggests that Asians are perceived as able, albeit not so able as whites. Afro-Caribbeans by contrast, particularly boys, are not thought of so positively. If the response to the former is to impose 'realism', for the latter it is to offer support and compensatory environments. Both strategies may inhibit achievement but Asians may be more likely to resist downward pressure on their aspirations. This is because their actual achievement levels are high. With Afro-Caribbeans, however, lower expectations and a 'welfare' approach may do more damage by confirming the apparent incapacity of the schools to capture the creative potential of Caribbean young people. (p83)

Others have also commented on differences in career aspirations among ethnic groups. Penn and Scattergood (1992) surveyed approximately 400 sixth formers in Rochdale in 1989, reporting that Asian respondents had very high aspirations.

The view forward for ethnic minority students from the end of compulsory education is likely to be shadowed by existing disadvantage, built into their academic attainment, and discrimination from various services and employers.

The situation by age 18

Drew et al (1992) concluded that by age 18, the ethnic minority groups were not short of educational qualifications but tended to show a different qualification profile from that of the white students, caused primarily by their Year 11 examination results. Turning to those who went directly into the youth labour market, they report that African-Caribbean young people were more likely than white young people to take up YTS places, having taken into account other factors such as educational attainment. They were also more likely to be unemployed and those who had been on YTS schemes were more vulnerable to unemployment than others. According to these analyses, black people were having particular trouble negotiating entry to the labour force. The African-Caribbean group lagged behind the rest in terms of the level of their age 16 educational qualifications, but even controlling for these differences it seemed that there were other barriers to their progress.

A recent Institute of Management Studies (IMS) report (Meager and Williams, 1994) claims that there is a strong economic case for addressing the problems that ethnic minorities face in entering the labour market. On average, ethnic minority groups account for over 5 per cent of the workforce, and this share will continue to rise due to the younger age structure of the ethnic minority population. Unemployment rates among these groups remain persistently about twice as high as white unemployment rates. There are however, considerable differences between ethnic groups, and also within the broader categories such as 'Asian'. Jones (1993) notes that ethnic differences in the overall unemployment rate are in fact magnified for the 16-24 age group, with young Pakistanis having an unemployment rate three times that of young whites, whilst young African-Asian men have a similar unemployment rate to their white counterparts. In January 1995, a written Parliamentary answer gave figures for unemployed young black men aged 16-24 as 62 per cent. Meager and Williams (1994) conclude that the evidence suggests that the main source of this disadvantage is not under-qualification on entry to the labour market, nor lack of training, but is due to discrimination in employment.

In conclusion, the evidence tends to point to an interaction of attainment, social contexts (including school) and discrimination in contributing to the relatively disadvantaged situation of many ethnic minority young people in their late teens. However, there are some limitations to the existing work on the role of ethnicity. The YCS cohorts are nationally representative and thus were not designed to explore the specific factors relevant to those leaving compulsory education in the inner cities. Some of the main reports (including *The Swann Report*) are now, given the pace of change in the market place, out of date.

The effects of multiple disadvantage

As Drew et al (1992) found, ethnic minority groups were over-represented in less privileged socio-economic groupings, were more likely to be from families headed by someone unemployed, and were most likely to be living in the inner cities. They were, thus, the most disadvantaged in the nationally representative study. That this is the case was emphasised recently by a CRE position paper on the Education Bill (CRE, 1993), which highlighted the dangers of a two-tier education system providing unequal access to quality provision. The CRE said:

> The existence of a differentiated system providing different levels of quality will be profoundly unfair for the parents who have no choice but to send their children to disadvantaged schools and of course will be profoundly unfair for the pupils themselves. Given the distribution of ethnic minority communities in the deprived areas of inner-cities and given the emerging trend that schools acquiring grant-maintained status are concentrated in suburban areas, it is likely that many ethnic minority children will be disproportionately represented in increasingly disadvantaged schools. (p6)

Some of the issues of multiple disadvantage are tackled by Connolly, Roberts, Ben-Tovim and Torkington (1992) who conducted an in-depth study of 'black youth' in Liverpool as part of the ESRC 16-19 Initiative. (Those who took part were not, however, from Asian, Chinese or other ethnic minority groups.) These young people, who left school in the mid 1980s, were faring worse not only than young Liverpudlians in general, but worse than the least qualified quarter. Only 37 out of 134 had ever been in regular full-time employment. Their parents had higher levels of unemployment than others in Liverpool, and fear of racial hostility was keeping the young people within their own district and social networks. They were more likely to have negative views of their schools, to have truanted regularly, and to have beliefs that further disadvantaged them. They believed, for example, that rejection by firms was inevitable, so they did not seek work as strenuously as others. The authors commented that much work was needed to depress the unemployment rate, as 'Many of the young people that we interviewed were too disillusioned and inhibited in their movements to take advantage of simple non-discrimination' (p94). They concluded that the next few years would be significant in determining whether this and subsequent generations of inner city black residents became a class apart – an underclass.

2

Methodology

The *Changing Lives* survey consisted of three waves of questionnaires sent to a large sample of 16 year olds during 1993-1994. The study focused on six urban areas in England where substantial proportions of the population belong to ethnic minority groups. *Changing Lives* was designed to be complementary to the Youth Cohort Survey (YCS) which is based on a nationally representative sample. *Changing Lives*, by contrast, concentrates on areas of high unemployment and poor living conditions. The design allowed us to describe in some detail the experiences of young people in these areas during the year following the end of their compulsory education, and to compare the experiences of different ethnic groups.

Study design

The core of this study involved a postal survey of young people from 34 schools in six urban areas. The pupils were in their final year of compulsory education at the beginning of 1993. The 34 schools were based in eight LEAs covering six TEC areas. The schools were chosen primarily with the aim of ensuring that the sample included a substantial proportion of young people (approximately half) from ethnic minority backgrounds. The areas were those covered by six TECs – London East, South Thames, Birmingham, Leeds, Manchester and Merseyside.

A range of different types and sizes of state school are represented among the 34, including 12 single-sex schools (nine all-girls and three all-boys). Eight of the schools were Voluntary Aided or Voluntary Controlled (including five Church of England schools and two Roman Catholic schools) and one school was Grant Maintained at the time of the study. Twenty of the schools had their own sixth form provision. All the schools were located in the inner cities, but a small minority of particularly popular schools had wide catchment areas that also included suburban areas.

All pupils who were eligible to leave the 34 schools during the spring or summer of 1993 (a total of 4,706) were sent the first questionnaire in September of that year. The second questionnaire was mailed to them in February 1994, and the third and final questionnaire was sent out in June 1994. The fact that the questionnaires were sent to the total population of Year 11 pupils that year makes the sample relatively unusual, in that there was no teacher selection. For example, in the YCS, head teachers were asked to consult with the eligible pupils and to pass on the names and addresses only of those willing to take part in the survey.

The *Changing Lives* questionnaires

The questionnaires were designed to be attractive to young people, and easy to read. This was very important given the inner city nature of the sample and the consequent likelihood that a small proportion would have reading problems. That we had some success in this respect was reflected in one response, where the respondent answered a question about ever having been treated unfairly by saying 'Yes – because I am dyslexic. This questionnaire was read to me and my answers marked down because of my handicap.' Piloting took place with sixth formers, college students, YT trainees and Careers Service clients. The three questionnaires had a core of common questions relating to current activity and satisfaction, the aim being to build up a longitudinal profile of respondents. In addition to this common element, each of the three questionnaires contained unique material, allowing a breadth of contextual data to be gathered over the year. While the first questionnaire focused to a certain extent on looking back to Year 11 at school, the second and third questionnaires gathered more information about current activities, social context and future plans. Table 2.1 presents an overview of the material included in each wave of data collection.

The same procedure was observed for each mailing. An initial copy of the questionnaire was followed by a reminder letter and a subsequent copy of the questionnaire for those who did not respond. A limited number of telephone interviews were also conducted with non-respondents. The intention here was again to take steps to reduce response bias resulting from non-completion of the written questionnaire by those young people who may have had literacy or language difficulties.

Table 2.1   Questionnaire content (summary)

Wave 1 Questionnaire 1 September 1993 covering	Wave 2 Questionnaire 2 February 1994 covering	Wave 3 Questionnaire 3 June 1994 covering
Core elements	*Core elements*	*Core elements*
Gender	Gender	Gender
Ethnicity	Ethnicity	Ethnicity
Monthly diary	Monthly diary	Monthly diary
Details of current occupation	Details of current occupation	Details of current occupation
Current happiness	Current happiness	Current happiness
Unique elements	*Unique elements*	*Unique elements*
Date of birth	Home responsibilities	Mother's occupation
Religion	Family attitudes	Father's occupation
Children	Family education	Living circumstances
Attitude to school	Problems faced	Attitudes to criminal
Absence from school	Sources of help	justice system
GCSE & other quals	Attitudes to education	Part-time work
Attitude to jobs & training		Year 11 decision in retrospect
Part-time activities		
Experience of discrimination		

The requirements of the Data Protection Act meant that in almost every case, schools were not able to give us the names and addresses of young people. Schools therefore mailed out questionnaires and re-minder letters on our behalf, using serial numbers to identify individual pupils. Many schools and Careers Services also assisted the researchers in obtaining permission from non-respondents for their telephone numbers to be released for follow-up interviews.

Respondents

The particular interest of *Changing Lives* was in exploring the effects of multiple disadvantage on the lives of young people in England today, and this was reflected in the choice of the sample. The *Changing Lives* sample was not selected in order to be broadly representative, either of all the young people in the six TEC areas from which it was drawn, or nationally; this is particularly true of the white young people in the sample. However, it was intended to represent young people from inner city areas and it was thus important to have as many people taking part at each wave as possible, so that we could be relatively confident about drawing conclusions.

Of the 4,706 pupils sent the first questionnaire, 2,955 completed questionnaires were received, 10 per cent of which were obtained through telephone interviews. This represents an overall response rate of 63 per cent. Response rates varied between schools from 34 per cent to over 90 per cent. In general, a higher than average response was obtained from all-girls schools and a lower than average response from all-boys schools. It was not possible to obtain telephone numbers of non-respondents from nine schools so, in these cases, no telephone interviews could be carried out.

The total group was sent the second questionnaire in February 1994, regardless of whether they had returned the first. A total of 2,539 returns were received, including 420 resulting from telephone follow-up of those who had not replied initially. The overall response rate to this second wave was 55 per cent. It is likely that some of this attrition is due to respondents changing address and consequently not receiving the questionnaire. The largest drop was in the Manchester area, partly due to one school failing to send out its questionnaires on time.

The third questionnaire, sent to the full sample in June 1994, resulted in the return of 2,429 questionnaires, representing a response rate of 52 per cent. Of these, 16 per cent were obtained through telephone interviews with those who had not responded to the postal survey. The response rate held up well, having only dropped by 3 per cent since the second survey.

Obviously, not everyone took part in all three waves. Indeed, some people only took part in one wave. In total, 3,608 people completed at least one questionnaire, a total response rate of 77 per cent. Figure 2.1 shows the various patterns of response that we had from the total sample.

A total of 1,670 people answered all three waves (35 per cent) but, given that the most important longitudinal analyses only required variables from Wave 1 and Wave 3, a total of 1,980 respondents were available for these analyses (42 per cent).

Figure 2.1   Patterns of sample response to the three waves of data collection

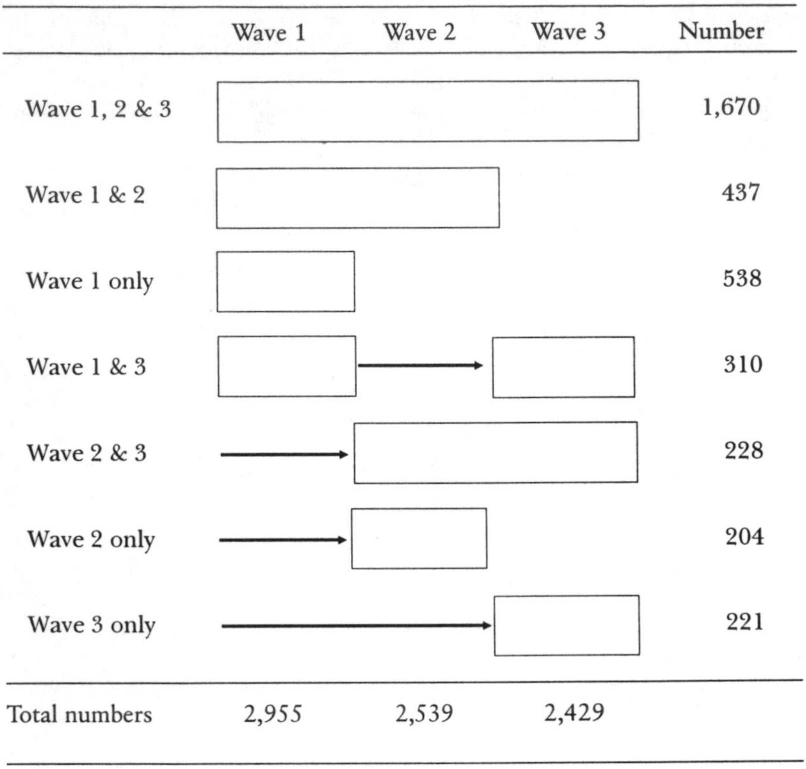

	Wave 1	Wave 2	Wave 3	Number
Wave 1, 2 & 3				1,670
Wave 1 & 2				437
Wave 1 only				538
Wave 1 & 3				310
Wave 2 & 3				228
Wave 2 only				204
Wave 3 only				221
Total numbers	2,955	2,539	2,429	

Four main sub-samples will be used in the analyses presented in this report:

(1) The Wave 1 sample, consisting of all those who responded to the first wave of the survey.

(2) The Wave 2 sample, consisting of all those who responded to the second wave, including those who did not respond to any or all the other waves.

(3) The Wave 3 sample, consisting of all those who responded to the third wave, including those who did not respond to any or all the other waves.

(4) The longitudinal sample, consisting of those who have data from at least both of Waves 1 and 3, and usually Wave 2 as well.

It is important to highlight the unusual nature of the *Changing Lives* sample, and who it can be said to represent. First, it targeted all of the eligible young people in Year 11 in the 34 schools and as such represents a total population sample of those schools in that year (given response bias). This is important because although the schools were selected because of certain characteristics, the young people were not further selected. Everyone in that year was sent a questionnaire. Second, the nature of the population living in the inner cities should be emphasised. Whilst most of Britain's ethnic minority population continues to live in inner urban areas, the same cannot be said of the white population. The young white people surveyed here are therefore in fact fairly *untypical* of white school leavers in the country as a whole. The ethnic minority samples are more representative (but not in any statistically valid sense) in having been drawn from inner-city schools. Third, it is important to note that each of the six areas covered by the study has unique demographic, labour market, education and training policy features and as such represents a unique environment. More attention will be given in the body of the report to the relative importance of the local environment in determining the nature of post-compulsory education transitions of young people. However, although each school comes from a delineated TEC area, it has to be remembered that the schools included in the study were located in particular localised districts (mainly those with high ethnic minority populations) and may not be typical of each TEC as a whole.

Thus, while it would not be justifiable to generalise the findings from this sample to the full population of 16 year olds, it is possible to draw some conclusions about the experiences of inner-city teenagers in the types of areas surveyed. It is also possible to examine and compare the experiences of different groups (for instance, females and males, those of different ethnic origins) who have previously shared a common education and are now subject to common post-16 opportunities and labour market conditions.

Sample non-response and attrition

Response bias in *Changing Lives* is potentially derived from two main sources:

1. *Initial response bias.* The overall response rates to the three sweeps were, respectively, 63, 55 and 52 per cent. Although these are reasonable for a postal survey with this type of sample, there was still a substantial number of people who did not reply. We know little of the characteristics of these non-respondents, but previous studies have found that the most disadvantaged groups are less likely to respond.

2. *Attrition from wave to wave within the study.* Fewer took part in each wave, and it is likely that those who dropped out differed from those who stayed in. However, due to the sample design, this was not as serious as it could have been. For the final report, the primary interest has to be in people who responded to all three waves (or at least to 1 & 3), but as Figure 2.1 showed, questionnaires were sent out to the total Wave 1 sample at Waves 2 and 3, even to non-respondents to the previous sweeps. This means that we have what the YCS call 'enhancement samples': people who responded, for example, to Wave 2 but not to any other. From this we can find out a little about attrition and also enhance the numbers for cross-sectional analyses, although these people cannot be used in the longitudinal analyses.

A number of variables were available at Wave 1 on respondents who then failed to take part in Waves 2 and 3 (type 2 above). From these it appeared that non-respondents to the later waves were significantly more likely to have lower or no GCSEs, to report more truancy, to be boys, to be from ethnic minorities and to be engaged in working or training rather than studying. They also reported that they were less happy than the rest with what they were doing at the time of the questionnaire. We can assume that non-respondents to the initial questionnaire at Wave 1 (type 1 above) would also have differed from respondents in the same sorts of ways. This sort of profile for non respondents is not unfamiliar and would be expected in a survey of this kind of sample.

Weighting

If a non-weighted sample is subjected to statistical analysis, each member of the sample has a default weight of 1 in the analyses – that is, they all count for the same. No one is more important than anyone else. However, if it is known that there are systematic biases in the sample, different weights can be assigned to sample members to correct for the biases. Thus, some members will have weights of more than one, some less than one. If successful, such a strategy will correct the sample back to the unbiased estimates.

A variety of types of information about non-respondents was available in *Changing Lives*. Information about the population was available from published data about the school examination results, and from interviews with the schools. Information about attrition from Wave 1 to Waves 2 and 3 was available from the Wave 1 data set. However, it was not possible to combine all the sources of information in order to weight the sample, because, for example, although there was an over-representation of young women among the respondents, and also an over-representation of people with better GCSE results, there was no population information available indicating how many of the latter would be expected to be young women. Similarly, although it was known that truants were under-represented in the later waves of the survey, and also that those with worse GCSE results were under-represented, the actual GCSE profiles of truants in the population were not known.

There was thus a choice. It was possible either to ignore the population data from the schools and weight Wave 3 back to Wave 1 but not account for the initial bias in Wave 1 respondents, or to weight each wave back to the population on a simple variable, but bypass the more sophisticated information available about non-response between the waves. The second method was the most straightforward, and had the advantage that we could then draw some conclusions about the inner-city population from which the sample was drawn. Otherwise, we may have internally adjusted for non-response from wave to wave but we would still have been left with the knowledge that the original sample was biased, which would restrict our licence to draw any broader conclusions.

The final situation was such that we knew quite a lot about who was not responding and who was not continuing to respond, but could only devise a simple weight to account for this. It was thus very important to pick the most significant variable on which respondents and non-respondents vary. Initial analyses looking both at initial response bias and between wave attrition suggested that one variable stood out above others, and also that this variable incorporated some of the others. This was pupils' GCSE results. Thus, comparing the school GCSE results for the year with those of respondents showed a consistent tendency for those with the better GCSEs to take part in the survey. Those with no GCSEs at all were under-represented. The magnitude of this tendency varies from school to school but the pattern was nearly always the same.

Similarly, looking at those who took part in Waves 1 and 3, compared with those who only took part in Wave 1, revealed that those who dropped out had significantly fewer GCSEs. The drop-outs also had higher truancy, were more likely to be from certain ethnic minorities, were more likely to be working or training at Wave 1 rather than studying, were less happy with what they were doing at Wave 1, and were more likely to be young men. A logistic regression, predicting participation in Wave 3 (or not), selected GCSEs as the most significant predictor. Once GCSEs, ethnicity and what respondents were doing at the time were in the model, there was no further effect for truancy, gender, or how happy respondents were.

Simply using GCSEs cannot account for ethnicity or current occupational differences, as these both had independent effects. However, since we did not know what the population GCSE results were that year for different ethnicities doing different things, it would not be possible to take these factors into account.

As both sets of comparisons pointed to the importance of GCSE results, specifically suggesting that it was the better qualified who were taking part, both initially and then in each subsequent wave, we decided to weight for GCSEs, back to the population as described in a full report of school examination results in the *Times* (17.11.93). Each respondent was given a score based on the three-way GCSE variable used to rate schools in the *Times*. Weights were then devised on a school by school basis. Thus, for example, the population (all Year 11 pupils) of the first school had rates of 25 per cent (5+ A-C grades), 61 per cent (1+ A-G grades), and 14 per cent (no GCSEs). The respondents from the first school had rates of 37 per cent (5+ A-C grades), 57 per cent (1+ A-G grades), and 6 per cent (no GCSEs). The first group was given a weight of less than 1, the middle group of approximately 1, and the last of over 1, to adjust these figures back to those for the school that year. Although the weight chosen is simple, the existence of a lot of other information about the drop-outs makes us reasonably confident that it is a good choice and will go some way to correcting for bias in the samples.

Four separate sets of weights based on GCSE results were calculated for use in the four sets of analyses to be included in this report:

1. Weighting Wave 1 back to the population, for use in cross-sectional analyses using only Wave 1 data (sample n2955).

2. Weighting Wave 2 back to the population, for use in cross-sectional analyses using only Wave 2 data (sample n2539, but only approximately 2,000 have wave 1 data with their GCSE results so the remainder keep a weight of 1).

3. Weighting Wave 3 back to the population, for use in cross-sectional analyses using only Wave 3 data (sample n2429, but only 1980 have wave 1 data with their GCSE results so the remainder keep a weight of 1).

4. Weighting the longitudinal sample (those with Waves 1 *and* 3) back to the population for use in longitudinal analyses (sample n1980).

Conclusion

The *Changing Lives* sample represents young people growing up in inner city areas and completing their full-time compulsory education in 1993. Although it would not be justifiable to generalise the findings from this sample to the full population of 16 year olds, it is possible to draw some conclusions about the experiences of inner-city teenagers in the types of areas surveyed. The sample was chosen to allow comparisons between different groups, such as young women and men, or different ethnic groups, who previously shared a common education and were then subject to common post-16 opportunities and labour market conditions.

Thirty-four schools took part. Altogether, 77 per cent of the young people finishing full-time education that year completed one of the *Changing Lives* questionnaires, and 35 per cent completed all of them. The sample was weighted to account for biases in responding.

Changing Lives 1, 2 and *3* (Shaw 1994a, Shaw 1994b, Shaw 1994c) presented cross-sectional results very swiftly after the end of each sweep of data collection. The main focus of this report, the last in the series, is on patterns over time, in terms of the broader context. In addition, we have included background material from the preliminary reports, in order that this report can stand alone as a full account of the results of the study. Although this leads to some overlap, the important distinction between the preliminary reports and this final report is that for the final report we have presented results based on weighted data, and thus patterns may vary slightly from those presented in the preliminary findings. The unweighted and weighted sample estimates for some of the major variables are presented in Appendix 2 to this report.

In the majority of the following tables, we have presented percentages in the body of each table, and weighted sample bases on the final line. Percentages have been rounded to the nearest whole number and thus may not always exactly total 100. For ease of reading, statistical test results are represented by the probability of a result occurring (the 'p' value), rather than detailed test results. Interested readers should contact the first author for further details.

3

The *Changing Lives* sample

Age and gender

The majority of the young people who took part were born between September 1976 and August 1977, and thus turned 16 between September 1992 and August 1993. Those who were already 16 by January 1993 reached the end of their compulsory education at Easter 1993. The remainder were entitled to leave school in the summer of 1993. During the year of the survey, 1993-1994, they were all over 16 and were, on average, 16 and a half years old.

The young women in the sample outnumbered the young men, with 57 per cent young women and 43 per cent young men responding to the first wave. The young women were then more likely to continue to take part, and by Wave 3 accounted for 59 per cent of the sample. The nationally representative YCS Cohort 5, who finished compulsory education in 1991, included 51 per cent young men, suggesting that young women were over-represented in the *Changing Lives* sample. Precise figures on sex ratios for each of the 34 schools were not available, so it is possible that the over-representation reflected a higher ratio of young women to young men in the original sample rather than simply response bias. However, it is known that young women tend to respond more readily to postal surveys and it is likely that at least some of the bias in the sex ratios was due to the fact that a higher proportion of the young women replied to the questionnaires.

The ratio of females to males remained fairly constant in each wave, with 43 per cent males in Wave 1, 40 per cent in Wave 2, and 41 per cent in both Wave 3 and the longitudinal sample (those who had completed all three questionnaires). The sex ratios varied by TEC area, so that in, for example, London East, there were approximately equal numbers of female and male respondents whereas in South Thames, there were far fewer male respondents compared with females. Figure

Figure 3.1   Gender by TEC area

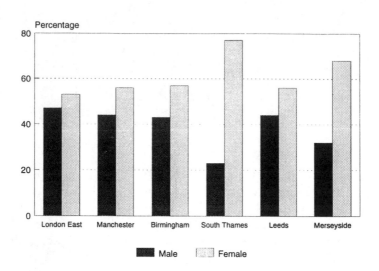

3.1 shows the gender by TEC pattern for the longitudinal sample. This confirms that there were larger proportions of young women than young men in all the TEC areas, and that the area where the ratio was smallest was London East.

Thus, different response rates for males and females and area variations accounted in part for the higher ratio of female respondents. In addition, there was a further reason for the over-representation of girls in the sample as a greater number of single-sex girls' schools were included in the study, in order to compensate for the known over-representation of boys in mixed schools. Both South Thames and Merseyside, for example, have two all-girls schools represented in their samples.

Ethnicity

At each wave, the ethnic categorisations used were those recommended by the Commission for Racial Equality and represent self-descriptions by the young people themselves. Where 'Other' or 'Black Other' were selected, a further description was requested. Four out of five of those selecting the category Black Other described themselves as being Black British, Black English or of mixed race. Those selecting Other also

Figure 3.2   Ethnic origin (longitudinal sample)

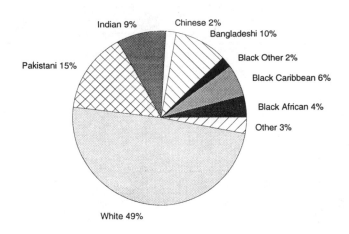

Weighted base, longitudinal sample, n=1,980

include those of mixed origins in addition to British Asians, those from Vietnamese, Middle Eastern, Arab and other European backgrounds.

Figure 3.2 shows the ethnic origin of the longitudinal sample, those who returned all three questionnaires, and Table 3.1 breaks down ethnic origin by TEC area for the longitudinal sample.

At all three waves, and in the longitudinal sample, we achieved the target of having around half of the respondents from minority ethnic groups. In total 51 per cent (of the longitudinal sample) belonged to an ethnic minority. The equivalent figures from the nationally representative YCS on young people who left compulsory education in 1991 (rather than 1993) suggests that 8.6 per cent of that cohort were not white (Courteney and McAleese, 1993). The YCS report did not provide a detailed breakdown of ethnicities, but did suggest that 1.3 per cent were black, 5 per cent were from Asian groups, 1 per cent were from other ethnic minorities, and 2 per cent did not state their ethnic origin. By providing a more detailed, and more recent, breakdown of ethnicity, the *Changing Lives* sample is thus unique. In both the YCS and the *Changing Lives* sample, Asian groups accounted for the majority of ethnic minority respondents.

Table 3.1 Ethnic origin by TEC area for the longitudinal sample

	Leeds	Man-chester	Mersey-side	Birm-ingham	London East	South Thames	All
Black African	1	5	5	1	4	7	4
Black Caribbean	2	9	0	9	5	20	6
Black Other	2	1	2	1	2	2	2
Bangladeshi	3	6	1	10	28	2	10
Chinese	1	2	2	<1	2	7	2
Indian	7	4	2	25	14	2	9
Pakistani	15	27	1	39	9	1	15
White	66	42	49	13	34	55	49
Other	3	5	2	3	3	6	3

Weighted base, longitudinal sample, n=1,980

The total proportions belonging to each group remained very similar over the three waves of data collection, although there were some small changes in the ethnic mix responding from each TEC area. However, attrition analyses presented in the previous chapter suggested that those dropping out from each wave were more likely to be from ethnic minorities, and it still remains the case that it is likely that the weighted data slightly under-represent the proportions from these groups in the 34 schools.

For some analyses it was necessary to use a summary ethnicity rating rather than the full coding, to maximise numbers. Dividing the sample on a three-way ethnicity variable resulted in 13 per cent Black (African/Caribbean/Other) 38 per cent Asian/Other (Bangladeshi, Chinese, Indian, Pakistani and Other) and 49 per cent white.

Living circumstances

As we would expect with a sample of this age, the majority of the respondents were living with their parents. Information about their living circumstances was only available for those who participated in Wave 3, and this suggests that 94 per cent were living with at least one parent. Table 3.2 presents the various different living circumstances reported by the respondents to the third questionnaire. The categories

Table 3.2   Living circumstances of the Wave 3 sample

Currently living with...	Per cent
Parents, +/- other siblings	94
Siblings only	1
Other relatives (+/- other siblings)	2
Partner (+/- own children)	1
Own children only	0
Friends/others	1
Alone	1
Total	100

in the table are exclusive. If respondents were living with a combination of people, priority was given to whether these included a parent.

Comparable figures were not presented in the YCS report on those leaving compulsory education in 1991, but the data suggest that 97 per cent were living with their parents, a slightly larger proportion than that found in *Changing Lives*. This could reflect the inner-city nature of the *Changing Lives* sample. In an inner-city area where multiple disadvantage is more likely to be present, a larger proportion of children will be living in non-traditional circumstances such as in Local Authority care. We know from another question in Wave 1 that 1 per cent had children of their own (two-thirds of whom were young women). This is a very small group, but larger than might be expected in a group of this age. If they already had a child by the first wave of data collection, the likelihood is that they conceived when they were under 16 years old. Census figures show less than five conceptions leading to a maternity per 1,000 girls aged 13-15 in 1991 (Central Statistical Office, 1994). According to this, we would expect a maximum of about ten young women with children in the *Changing Lives* sample, whereas the (weighted) figure is 18 young women and nine young men.

We do not know how many of those who reported living with parents were living with a lone parent. Defining living with a lone parent is very difficult, and many families operate complicated custody patterns involving some care by both parents. Asking respondents to self-define their situation was likely to lead to non-comparable definitions being used.

If the data on living circumstances are broken down by gender, it appears that all of those living with their partners and/or their own children were young women. In fact, the young men were slightly more likely to be living with their parents than the young women were. Seven per cent of the young women were living in some other situation compared with 5 per cent of the young men. Although the numbers were very small, young women were more likely than young men to be living with other relatives, with friends, or alone.

In terms of ethnic patterns, the picture was not entirely straightforward. The Asian groups were most likely to be with their parents, with 95 per cent of Bangladeshi, 99 per cent of Indian and 97 per cent of Pakistani young people doing so, compared with 94 per cent of the white young people. The exception to this was the Chinese young people, of whom 93 per cent were living with a parent. Young people from black families were far less likely than the other groups to be living with their parents, with 81 per cent of the Black Africans and 84 per cent of the Black Caribbeans doing so. An exception to this was the Black Other group, of whom 97 per cent were living with a parent. Numbers of respondents in the Black Other and Chinese categories were the smallest, with only 29 in the former group and 40 in the latter (weighted), so these figures should be treated with caution. It seems likely that the overall pattern is of Asian families being most likely to keep their children at home with their parents, and Black young people being most likely to have left home, or to have alternative living arrangements.

None of the young people with children living as lone parents were from the Asian groups, and only one of the 15 young people living with their partners was from an Asian group, the remainder of these people being either white or from black ethnic groups. Neither were Asians represented amongst the group of 13 young people living on their own.

Looking at patterns by TEC area, the South Thames and Manchester areas had the lowest rate of young people living with their parents (91 per cent and 92 per cent respectively) and Birmingham the highest (97 per cent). This almost certainly reflects the ethnic composition of the samples from the different areas, as the Asian groups were most highly represented in the Birmingham TEC, and the Black groups in the South Thames area.

34

Family background

A person's aspirations and expectations are likely to be shaped in part by their parents' occupations, and it was important to collect some information about parental background in the questionnaires. However, in piloting the questionnaires, we found this to be a sensitive subject, both to those no longer in touch with one or both natural parents, and to those who did not appreciate the relevance of the questions. For this reason, we left questions about family background until the final questionnaire, and phrased the questions as sensitively as possible, explaining their purpose and emphasising that 'parent' could mean whoever the respondent thought of as a parent, be they biological, step, adoptive or foster parents. Figures presented in this section again refer to the weighted Wave 3 respondents.

Whether or not a parent has a degree is often taken as a crude indicator of family educational aspirations. The minority of the parents in the *Changing Lives* study had been educated to degree level. Nine per cent of the mothers and 10 per cent of the fathers had degrees, with higher rates among the Black African families (27 per cent of the mothers, 32 per cent of fathers). Those from the Asian groups had the lowest rates (approximately 1 per cent for parents in Bangladeshi families, 2 per cent for parents in Chinese families). The rates for the white families were 12 per cent of mothers and 14 per cent of fathers.

Turning to occupational ratings, *Changing Lives 3* reported that just over half of the respondents' mothers had worked in the last five years, as had nearly two thirds of the fathers. On the basis of information collected in the third questionnaire, a five-way summary rating of socio-economic status was calculated, splitting the families into those with non-manual backgrounds, skilled manual, semi or unskilled manual, self employed and not working (the majority of whom were either unemployed, caring or disabled). Lack of any relevant information meant that this could not be calculated for 5 per cent of respondents to the third wave. The classifications of the remainder are presented in Figure 3.3. In cases where information was missing on fathers, details from the mother were substituted. If information about both mother's occupation and father's in the last five years was missing, but it was known that neither parent was working at the time that the questionnaire was completed, a coding of 'not working' was substituted. In this way, priority was given to information about the father stretching back five years, but maximum use was made of other available details as well.

Figure 3.3   Family socio-economic status rating

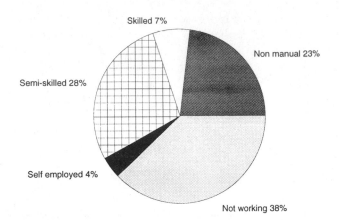

Weighted base, Wave 3, n=2,268

The figure demonstrates that the largest sections of the sample came either from families where the head was not working, or from the semi/unskilled sector. Together these accounted for 66 per cent of the respondents. It is likely that a proportion of the families classified as not working will be lone mother families. The third largest classification was non-manual, including both professional and all other non-manual occupations. Reflecting the changes in the economic and labour base of inner-city areas over the last 50 years or so, only 7 per cent came from skilled manual backgrounds. Self employment was also very low at 4 per cent.

Comparisons of socio-economic status by ethnicity suggest that the highest rates of not working came in the Asian groups, with 75 per cent of Bangladeshi families, 56 per cent of Chinese families, 38 per cent of Indian families and 54 per cent of Pakistani families not working, compared with rates of between 33 and 45 per cent of the Black families and 20 per cent of the white families. The highest rates of non-manual occupations came within the white families. Thus the white young people in the sample are doubly advantaged compared with their ethnic minority counterparts in that not only are they considerably more likely to have a working parent, but their parent is also more likely to be working in a higher status (non-manual) occupation than a working parent of an ethnic minority respondent.

Conclusion

One of the key issues that underpinned the *Changing Lives* study was the recognition that there remain significant inequalities of opportunity in education, training and work. To explore these issues, we focused particularly on the different experiences of young men and women from urban areas.

The respondents in the *Changing Lives* study were, on average, $16\frac{1}{2}$ years old. They came from a range of schools in a range of areas, but overall the inner-city nature of the sample selection was reflected in their basic demographic profile. Half came from ethnic minorities, mostly from Asian groups. A slightly higher proportion than we might expect from national statistics were not living with their parents. Only a minority had parents with degrees, and most came from semi- and unskilled backgrounds or from households where their parents were not working. As expected, in socio-economic terms, the *Changing Lives* sample were less well off than might have been expected in repre-sentative groups of this age and, within this sample, young people from Black or Asian backgrounds were particularly disadvantaged.

4

Looking back at school

As the National Commission on Education noted (1993, p151), 'self-esteem, attitudes towards school work, and educational aspirations are all connected with achievement'. As the Commission went on to point out, however, the public perception that schools are full of disenchanted pupils is some distance from the truth. The Commission's own survey found that the majority of pupils demonstrated strong support for the value of schools and researchers from Keele University found that 88 per cent of pupils are usually happy in school (Barber, undated). Nevertheless, as Barber says, 'for many young people in this country, school, particularly the secondary phase, fails to inspire. For some young people this is a gross understatement. These are the ones who have opted out of school entirely'.

Regardless of their destination at age 16, the *Changing Lives* sample were asked to look back at the last year of their compulsory education (Year 11) and report on their academic and vocational qualifications achieved at school, their attitudes to school in general and beliefs about education, reasons for absence from school, and the quality of careers advice received. Questions about education were included both in Waves 1 and 2 (all three questionnaires are reproduced in Appendix 4).

Examination achievement

The majority of the young people in the study took GCSEs, and a minority also or alternatively took vocational qualifications. Figure 4.1 presents a summary rating of GCSE attainment for the whole *Changing Lives* sample. The five categories are exclusive, and give priority to any A-C grades. Thus, an individual with seven GCSE passes, two at grade C and five at grade D would be placed in the 1-4 A-C category. The

Figure 4.1   Year 11 GCSE attainment

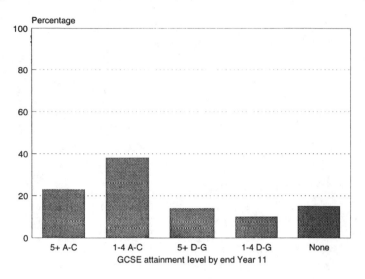

Weighted base, Wave 1, n=2,955

figure shows that nearly a quarter achieved five or more high-graded GCSEs, 38 per cent achieved between one and four high-graded GCSEs, 14 per cent got five or more lower graded results, 10 per cent got between one and four lower graded results, and 15 per cent did not achieve any grades at GCSE at all.

According to Department for Education (DfE) Statistical Bulletin 7/94, reporting the national GCSE results for 1993, 41 per cent of young people had achieved five or more passes at grades A to C and only 7 per cent failed to achieve any passes at grades A to G. Thus, the *Changing Lives* sample were underachieving in comparison to national statistics, as we would have expected.

Also as expected, the level of qualification attained varied by gender, and by ethnicity. This is illustrated using a simple scale based on the categories outlined in Figure 4.1. Each respondent was allocated a score from 1 to 5, so that 1 represents no GCSE passes at all, 2 represents one to four passes at grade D or below only, 3 represents five or more passes all at grade D or below, 4 represents one to four passes at grade C or above, and 5 represents five or more passes at grade C or above. Confirming virtually all recent reports of comparisons between girls

Figure 4.2   Comparing Year 11 GCSE attainment by ethnic group

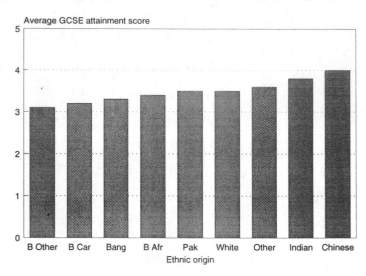

Weighted base, Wave 1, n=2,955 (F=5.35, df 2898,8, p<.001)

See note 1, p110

and boys (eg. DfE, June 1994, Payne, 1995a), we found a statistically significant relationship between gender and academic achievement, with young women scoring an average of 3.6 on this GCSE scale compared with 3.3 for the young men (p<.001).

GCSE attainment also varied significantly by ethnic group, as Figure 4.2 shows. The graph compares the average scores on the Year 11 GCSE scale for each ethnic group.

The highest achieving groups were the Chinese and Indian students, and the lowest the Black Other and Black Caribbean groups. The YCS report on nationally representative young people in 1991 states that ethnic minority members had lower Year 11 attainment levels than whites although there was considerable diversity of attainment levels between different ethnic minorities (Courtney and McAleese, 1993). From the *Changing Lives* results, it is obviously very important to bear these differences in mind as, in fact, *both* the highest and the lowest achieving groups were ethnic minority groups. It is also worth noting the marked differences in achievement of those minority groups of

Table 4.1   GCSE results by TEC area, compared with LEA figures

Percentages

	Rates of 5+ GCSEs grades A-C		Rates of 1+ GCSEs grades A-G	
	In *Changing Lives*	In the local LEA*	In *Changing Lives*	In the local LEA
Leeds	27	34	83	90
Manchester	22	21	83	80
Merseyside	28	25	84	84
Birmingham	15	27	90	88
London East	20	21	85	87
South Thames	25	23	86	84

Weighted base, Wave 1, n=2,955

* See note 2, p110

Asian origin, whereby Bangladeshi young people achieved less well than their white counterparts, respondents of Pakistani origin at roughly the same level, and Chinese and Indian groups out-performed all their contemporaries. Other research reports from PSI have emphasised ethnic diversity and emerging and evolving plurality within 'Britishness' (Modood, Beishon and Virdee, 1994, Modood and Shiner, 1994).

Despite the fact that both were significant predictors of GCSE score on their own, a statistical test for an interaction between gender and ethnicity was not significant. This result suggested that there were no groups of young men or young women from particular ethnic groups within the *Changing Lives* sample who performed especially well or badly at GCSE.

How did the examination results of the *Changing Lives* sample compare to those of other young people in their local areas? Table 4.1 presents the comparison of the weighted figures for the *Changing Lives* sample with the published Local Education Authority figure for each of the TECs, showing the extent to which the young people were typical of those in their local authority in terms of academic achievement.

The percentage achieving five or more A to C grade GCSEs in each area was approximately similar to those of the LEAs as a whole, with the exception of Birmingham, where the *Changing Lives* sample significantly underachieved in comparison to their area. Those in the Leeds area also underachieved but to a lesser extent. In Birmingham, all the schools in the study fell in the lower half of the LEA 'league table'. However, the rates of those in Birmingham achieving at least one G grade were approximately the same as for that LEA as a whole, suggesting that rates of taking at least some GCSEs were the same, but that the *Changing Lives* sample were not achieving the higher grades. For all the areas, the table confirms that, like most young people in their locality, the vast majority of young people in the sample achieved at least one G grade.

Not surprisingly, there was a strong association between the school attended and the students' attainment levels ($p < .001$). Of the five schools with the highest levels, three were all-girls schools (the remainder mixed), and most came in the top third of their area's league placings. Of those five schools with the lowest levels, two were all-boys (the remainder mixed), and most came in the bottom third of the local league placings.

Twelve per cent of the sample had also taken at least one non-GCSE qualification, such as City and Guilds, RSA, BTEC or NPRA, alongside or instead of GCSEs. The comparable figure in the national YCS two years earlier was 11 per cent. This figure was falling from year to year and is likely to be much lower in the latest YCS cohorts on whom data is not yet published. We would expect higher rates among an inner city sample from largely semi- or unskilled backgrounds, as family and local investment in vocational options are likely to be higher than in more academic and privileged groups.

Experiences of school

'I never liked school,' wrote an apprentice welder and steel fabricator, 'and I am happy to be at work. I have been more successful than any of my teachers said I would be.' In fact, only the minority of respondents felt this way, but it was clear that attitude to school was related to academic achievement. Questions in the first wave invited young people to look back over their years of compulsory schooling and offered three statements with which to agree or disagree. The first statement was *School has made me feel I have something to offer*, the second was *School has been a waste of time* and the third *School has taught me things which would be useful in a job*.

The overall response to these questions showed very positive attitudes towards school with little variation between male and female

Figure 4.3   Attitude to school, by ethnicity

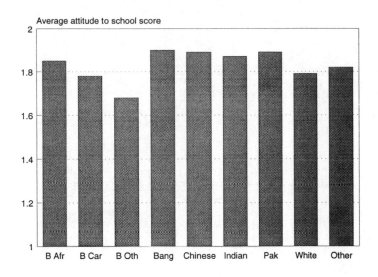

Average attitude to school score

Weighted base, Wave 1, n=2,955 (F=10.17, df 2634,8, p<.001)

respondents. Black Caribbean, Black Other and white ethnic groups were slightly less satisfied than other ethnic groups.

In order to relate their feelings about school to other factors such as their academic achievement, a scale of 'Attitude to school' was devised, taking an average of their responses to these three questions. The scale was constructed so that a high score reflected a positive attitude. Results from this clearly demonstrated that most of the *Changing Lives* respondents felt positively about their schools. The average score on this scale (which could potentially range from 1, negative, to 2, positive) was 1.8.

There was a significant effect for ethnicity on this scale, and as Figure 4.3 demonstrates, the groups who reflected most positively about school were the Asian groups, while those with the most negative impressions of school were the Black groups. The white respondents fell in the middle. There were, however, no gender effects, both young men and young women averaging 1.8.

Although the average scores for each of the six areas looked reasonably similar, ranging from 1.82 for London East, to 1.78 for South Thames, in fact the differences were statistically significant, with the young people in some areas reporting more negative views of the value

Figure 4.4   Attitude to school, by GCSE attainment

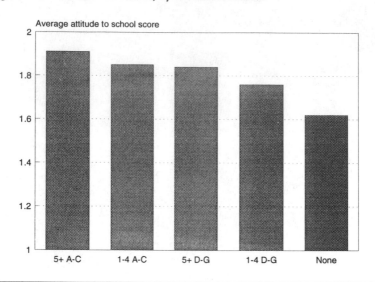

Weighted base, Wave 1, n=2,955 (F=10.17, df 2634,8, p<.001)

of their schools than those in other areas (p<.02). These differences did not seem to be related to the relative league positions of the schools within their TECs – as we saw earlier, many of the schools in the Birmingham TEC were placed in the bottom third of the LEA league table, yet the young people in Birmingham scored an average of 1.83, the second most positive school rating found among the TECs. It should be recalled, however, that the TECs varied in terms of the ethnic mix of the sample, and it is likely that area differences partly reflect these. Both the London East and Birmingham sample contain relatively high proportions of young people from Asian ethnic groups.

However, despite the fact that the area differences were not explained by the relative league positions of the school in the different areas, there *were* strong school effects (p<.001), presumably related to other factors apart from the league status of the school. There were no obvious similarities among the five schools whose pupils reported the most positive views. They included representatives from throughout the league tables, including both one from the top and one from the bottom. Two were all-girls and the remainder were mixed. Those five with the least positive ratings all came from the bottom of their local league tables, and included one all-boys school. The remainder were mixed. The emerging pattern for all-boys schools to do relatively badly on a range of variables, and all-girls schools to do relatively well, is very interesting, but these data do not allow for any further analysis. However, as we know that there were no overall gender differences in the 'Attitude to school' index, the fact that the top five include a girls school (but no boys schools) and the bottom five include two boys schools (but no girls schools) cannot be attributed simply to gender differences.

Presumably these school differences reflect complex factors related to the atmosphere and ethos of each school. Research on school differences (eg. Rutter et al, 1979) has suggested that secondary schools have an effect on a range of individual factors such as achievement and attendance and that these stem from features such as the social organisation of the school and the nature of the pupil-staff relationships.

At an individual level, it was clear that perceptions of the value of school were related to the respondent's GCSE results. Although not huge (.3), the correlation between the two was strongly significant ($p<.001$). The relationship is pictured in Figure 4.4, showing that the higher a pupil's GCSE scores, the more positively they felt about school in general.

Missing school

The significance of truancy as a factor affecting subsequent labour market performance has been highlighted in a YCS analysis of data relating to young people eligible to leave school in 1990. Casey and Smith (1995) found that, even after allowing for the effects of exam performance and social background, a high level of truancy in Year 11 was strongly associated with poor labour market outcomes, such as unemployment, in the following three years. Those who had truanted in Year 11 were more likely to have parents belonging to lower occupational groups, to live in council accommodation and to be living with one or neither of their parents. Black young people were more likely to have truanted than other ethnic groups.

In a recent study for the Department for Education, O'Keefe (1993) found that just under a third of 14 and 15 year olds admitted having truanted at least once in the previous half term, 18 per cent at least once a month, and 8 per cent at least once a week. Interestingly, he found no marked differences between boys and girls, except for truancy in

Figure 4.5   Truancy in Years 10 and 11, by ethnicity

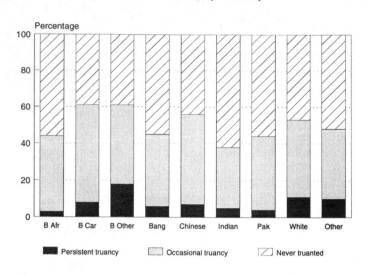

Weighted base, Wave 1, n=2,955 (F=10.17, df 2634,8, p<.001)

Year 11. There was some evidence that living in the inner city was influential – the mean absence level in schools where the headteacher said there were no pupils from the inner city was 13.6 per cent, whereas it was 26.3 per cent in schools where headteachers said more than half of the pupils lived in the inner city. Unfortunately, O'Keefe was not able to present any data on the experiences of pupils of different ethnic origins.

The first report, *Changing Lives 1,* had reported that around half (47 per cent) of the sample had truanted at some time or other during Years 10 and 11. Weighting for non-response increased this proportion to 50 per cent. A third of the sample had missed odd days or lessons (32 per cent), a tenth had missed particular lessons or days (10 per cent), and the remainder had missed either several days at a time (4 per cent) or weeks at a time (also 4 per cent). It was thus far from unusual for members of the *Changing Lives* sample to miss school although truanting for days or weeks at a time was relatively rare.

A summary three-way truancy variable, split into persistent truancy, occasional truancy and no truancy, where days and weeks at a time both represent persistent truancy, showed that the *Changing Lives* proportions were 8 per cent persistent, 42 per cent occasional and 50 per cent no truancy. Figure 4.5 shows these broad truancy categories broken down by ethnicity for the *Changing Lives* sample.

The figure shows some differences between ethnic groups, with Asian and Black African groups being least likely to have truanted during their last two years at school. Indian respondents were least likely to have done so, 62 per cent stating that they had never truanted. Black Caribbean and Black Other groups were most likely to have missed some school due to truancy, over 60 per cent admitting to this in each case. We have already seen that these two groups had a somewhat less positive attitude to school and lower achievement at GCSE than other ethnic groups. Respondents describing themselves as Black Other were markedly more likely than the sample as a whole to have truanted for days or weeks at a time, 18 per cent having done so.

Perceptions of the relevance of school

In the second wave, approximately nine months after the end of their compulsory education, respondents were asked whether they agreed or disagreed with a set of eight statements about young people, work and employment. Several of these focused again on school and qualifications, and their relevance to future prospects. Their responses to these statements are presented in Figure 4.6; the remainder of the statements will be analysed separately in Chapter 8 ('Experiences, attitudes and aspirations'). The figure compares percentages of the sample agreeing with each of six statements broken down by GCSE results.

Perhaps one of the more interesting features of Figure 4.6 is the degree of agreement on certain issues between those with different levels of qualification at GCSE. This is perhaps most striking in the case of the final statement, *Failure in examinations ruins a person's chances in life*, those who have in fact already failed being no more likely than those who have succeeded to agree with this statement. However, the majority of the sample, regardless of qualifications, acknowledge that *Employers pay a lot of attention to school reports and examination results*, and around half believe that having the right contacts and going to the right school are important factors in a young person's success in the job market.

Where there is a more noticeable difference between the high and low achievers, those without GCSE passes are more likely to have a broadly fatalistic outlook. For example, three fifths of those without

Figure 4.6   The relevance of school to work by GCSE attainment

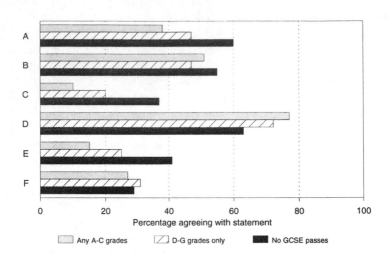

Key to statements

A   'It is mainly a matter of luck whethera school-leaver gets a job or not'

B   'Going to the right school and having the right contacts is a big part of getting a job'

C   'It really doesn't matter how well you do at school'

D   'Employers pay a lot of attention to school reports and examination results'

E   'Some people require education for their jobs but for most of us it is a waste of time'

F   'Failure in examination ruins a person's chances in life'

Weighted base, Wave 2, n=2,029

qualifications agree that *It is mainly a matter of luck whether a school-leaver gets a job or not*. This group is also almost four times as likely to agree with the statement, *It really doesn't matter how well you do at school*, than those with at least one high grade GCSE pass.

Careers advice

'I don't think', wrote one pupil, 'that my school gave me the sufficient knowledge for when I left school, for example, careers, opportunities, life.' The quality of careers advice varies considerably, and can be

Figure 4.7   Relative helpfulness of various sources of careers advice

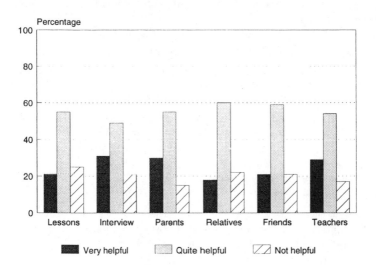

received in a variety of ways, both formal (such as in timetabled careers lessons or interviews with careers officers) and informal (for instance, by talking with friends and family members). The first questionnaire asked what types of advice respondents had had, and how helpful each had been.

Background information, collected in interviews with representatives of the different schools themselves, had revealed many ways in which careers education was delivered within the schools. This could range from a flourishing department with a full programme of activities, to an occasional session with a non-specialist teacher, according to the policy and resources of each school. In addition, the 34 schools in the study were served by eight Careers Services (external to the school) all with their own policies for delivering advice.

Respondents from different schools gave very varying reports of the usefulness of the services provided both by their school and by their Careers Service. For those who used each source of advice, their assessments of the relative helpfulness of a range of sources of careers advice are shown in Figure 4.7. The most common forms of advice for people to have had were careers lessons at school and an interview with the careers officer. Ninety per cent of the sample had attended a lesson at school, and over 90 per cent had had an interview with a careers officer from the local Careers Service. Talking to relatives was relatively rare, with approximately 60 per cent of the sample having used this source of advice.

Only around a fifth of all pupils found careers lessons to have been 'very helpful', although over half thought they had been 'quite helpful'. The differences between the schools were considerable, with the proportions having found such lessons to have been 'very helpful' ranging from 5 per cent to 56 per cent (p<.001). In terms of the sessions provided by the Careers Service, generally these were seen to have been rather more helpful, a third of the sample rating them as 'very helpful', and a further third finding them quite helpful. The responses vary by area, respondents in Birmingham and London East being most favourable about their local service, and those in Merseyside and Leeds being least positive (p<.01).

Informal sources, such as talks with other teachers at school, or with family members, were often rated as being as helpful as the formal service provided by the school, although if the 'very helpful' responses are compared, they were generally not quite as useful as a formal Careers Service interview.

To explore ethnicity differences, the information was summarised so that both 'very helpful' and 'quite helpful' were combined into one category of 'helpful', and the opinions of each of the different ethnic groups were compared for each type of careers advice. The results are shown in Table 4.2, which also divides the types of careers advice into formal and informal.

The overall impression gained from Table 4.2 is that the young people in the sample found a wide range of sources of careers advice to be helpful. Examining the table more closely, however, reveals some differences between ethnic groups. For instance, the Bangladeshi group were particularly likely to have found formal sources of advice helpful, relying less on their family and friends. This may be related to the fact that many of the Bangladeshi young people in the sample were not born in the UK and would therefore be less likely to have relatives and friends with knowledge and experience of further and higher education or the local labour market options. By contrast, the Black Other group, who we have already seen to be somewhat less positive about school than many other ethnic groups, find family and friends considerably more helpful than careers officers or careers lessons.

Space was allowed at the end of the questionnaires for respondents to add any comments, and many made reference to careers information

Table 4.2   Helpfulness of various sources of careers advice by ethnicity

Percentages finding each source helpful

	Formal advice		Informal advice			
	School	Careers	Family	Relatives	Friends	Teachers
Black African	69	77	86	84	83	78
Black Caribbean	79	84	84	80	75	82
Black Other	69	63	88	88	80	83
Bangladeshi	90	87	83	83	87	92
Chinese	72	79	70	69	80	76
Indian	83	82	83	77	75	86
Pakistani	86	82	83	77	87	90
White	69	76	87	75	77	79
Other	66	78	83	81	71	78

Weighted bases, Wave 1, range from 1,593 to 2,541

Comparisons only include people who said they used each advice source

at this point. Generally, these were on the negative side, as those who had rated services positively presumably did not feel it necessary to add any further explanation. A random selection of comments suggested that one theme emerging was the tendency of advice to centre on staying on at school rather than going to college. Hence, one respondent wrote, 'Schools should make information about college courses, GNVQs and training schemes much more readily available, instead of just giving the impression that you stay on to the sixth form, or you leave and get a job.' Similarly, another commented 'I believe I should have been given more information from my school about colleges. They pushed the school 6th form with me, which is what I chose, and I now regret my choice as I feel as if I am not treated with as much respect as I would be in a college.'

Conclusion

As we expected, the *Changing Lives* sample achieved fewer GCSEs at the higher grades than national samples in the same year, although most achieved at least one low-graded GCSE. In fact, comparing the examination results of the respondents with those of all young people in the LEAs showed that although the *Changing Lives* respondents were not achieving the higher grades, at least as many managed to achieve the lower grades. Various factors seemed to be related to achievement. The young women scored better, as did those from certain ethnic groups and those who went to certain schools.

As other studies have indicated, good GCSE results are of crucial importance in the route beyond compulsory education. Payne (1995a) showed that in the YCS, academic attainment in the form of GCSEs was the biggest single influence on staying-on rates, and was also strongly related to success in both further education and vocational options post-16. Kerckhoff (1990) reported similar trends for the NCDS in the 1970s. It is already obvious that the inner-city sample that took part in *Changing Lives* were starting their post-compulsory education pathways at a disadvantage, this being particularly true of the young men.

The mixture of positive and negative experiences during their school years was an interesting feature of the results. Overall, the sample reported higher truancy rates than those reported for national samples, suggesting less attachment to school and academic achievement generally. However, most respondents reported fairly positive views of school, and those who had taken up opportunities for receiving careers advice had found this helpful.

5

Initial destinations at age 16

The main aim of the study was to examine the transitions experienced by the sample of 16 and 17 year olds and to follow their paths from Year 11 into further education, training and work. The next three chapters explore these transitions. First, in this chapter, we look at the initial destinations of sample members at the end of their last year of compulsory schooling. Second, in Chapter 6, we track the various different pathways taken by sample members after that initial starting point, through the rest of Year 12. Most of this information comes from questions asking respondents to account for their main activities on a monthly basis throughout Year 12. Finally, in Chapter 7, we explore ways of identifying those sample members most likely to follow different pathways or end up in certain places, the aim being to predict who will go which way.

Destinations at age 16

Students were expected to be employed in a variety of activities over the summer months, and so their destinations at 16 were assessed in September 1993, when those who were starting new courses, for example, might have been expected to have begun. The respondents were given seven main options, including full-time study, training or work, unemployment, waiting for a job, waiting for Youth Training, or 'Other'. The two 'waiting' categories indicated those who had been offered a job but had not yet started, and those who were waiting to be allocated a training place. The term 'unemployed', as used in this research, represents the young person's own interpretation of their situation; consequently these figures should not be compared directly with those from other sources which may use different definitions. It

should be noted that 16 and 17 year olds are not included in official unemployment figures.

As expected, the majority of the students opted to stay in some form of education at 16. Table 5.1 shows the destinations of the respondents presented by area.

Table 5.1   Destinations of respondents in September 1993

	f-t study	f-t training	f-t work	unem- ployed	wait - job	wait - YT	other things
Leeds	76	8	8	5	1	1	2
Manchester	78	6	4	7	1	2	3
Merseyside	73	14	5	7	0	1	1
Birmingham	75	9	4	5	2	4	1
London East	77	9	6	5	1	1	2
South Thames	75	6	4	10	0	3	4
Total	76	9	5	6	1	2	2
Weighted base	*2,158*	*243*	*153*	*174*	*18*	*49*	*57*

At first glance, the table reflects little difference between the TEC areas. In each of the areas, approximately three quarters of the sample were in full-time education. Respondents who were not studying were most likely to be training (or waiting for training to start).

The numbers falling into the last four categories on the table were small, so these were amalgamated into one 'Other' category. Further statistical analysis showed that there were, in fact, significant differences between destinations of young people in the different areas, despite the overall similarity in pattern (p < .001). Levels of participation in training were highest in the area with the most depressed local labour-market (Merseyside), and unemployment was also higher in this area and another with a depressed local market (South Thames). Apart from these simplistic observations, it is not easy to know what to attribute these area differences to. A number of additional factors could be driving these TEC differences including differences in careers service provision and policy, individual marketing campaigns by colleges or training providers, and differences in schools between TEC areas. More information would be needed to untangle these patterns, but it is important to note the role of the TEC areas in investigating destinations at 16.

Comparing the destinations of the *Changing Lives* samples with those of their national peers is also a little difficult because classifications of definitions vary between, for example, *Changing Lives* and the YCS and data from the same year are not available. However, the categories used by the Careers Service in their report on the destinations of school leavers in 1993 (Yates, 1994) are very similar to those used in *Changing Lives*, the main difference being the category Unemployed, which includes other activities. The Careers Service has data on all but 6 per cent of this age group in England and Wales. Table 5.2 compares the overall destinations of the *Changing Lives* sample with those known to the Careers Service in England and Wales. The Careers Service data have been adjusted to reflect the known destinations of the 94 per cent of young people for whom they had information.

Table 5.2 Comparison of *Changing Lives* destinations at 16 and those known to the Careers Service

	Changing Lives Sept 1993	*Changing Lives* Feb 1994	Careers Autumn 1993
Full-time education	76	71	73
Full-time work	5	6	8
Training Scheme	9	9	13
Unemployed	6	8	6
Other	4	5	n/a
Weighted base	*2,851*	*2,537*	

The *Changing Lives* full-time education figures began by being higher than those reported by the Careers Service. By February 1994, the *Changing Lives* figure had dropped to just below the Careers Service figure, but remains very comparable. From this it appears that the *Changing Lives* sample were equally likely to be in full-time education (despite the fact that their overall Year 11 examination results lagged some way behind those for the national Careers Service sample). Later sections will track pathways throughout the year.

Comparisons with the national statistics suggest that even for an inner-city 16 year old with depressed levels of educational attainment, full-time education is as much of an option as it is to the average 16 year old in the UK. These findings raise several questions which will be returned to in further analyses. An important issue is the *types* of full-time education that these students are pursuing – given the lower level of academic attainment, these are likely to vary from those pursued by their representative peers.

Gender and ethnicity differences in initial destinations at 16

It has been suggested that more young women than young men stay on in full-time education in the period immediately after the end of compulsory education, partly because they continue with education in order to take clerical and business courses (Banks et al, 1992). We found that the young women in the *Changing Lives* sample were, indeed, more likely to go straight into studying; 78 per cent compared with 73 per cent of the young men (p<.01). Their destinations are compared in Figure 5.1.

Figure 5.1   Initial destinations at age 16 by gender

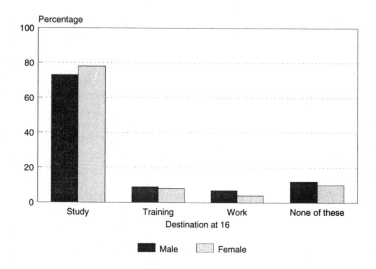

Weighted base, Wave 1, n=2,840

Figure 5.2   Initial destinations at 16 by ethnicity

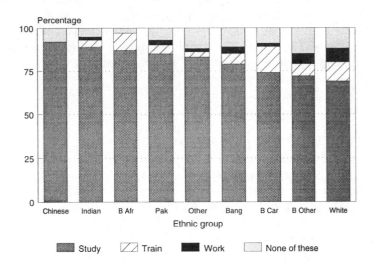

If they did stay on in education at age 16, the young women were more likely to be doing their studying at their old schools (39 per cent, compared with 28 per cent of the young men) whereas the young men were more likely to have moved on to a college of further education (43 per cent, compared with 31 per cent of the young women). Not all the schools in the study had sixth form provision (13 schools did not), but those that did included both single-sex boys' and girls' schools. However, despite the fact that they tended to be studying in different places, there were few indications that there were differences in the qualifications for which they were studying. Of the people who (a) were staying on in education and (b) told us what they were studying for, slightly fewer young women than men were studying for vocational qualifications (37 per cent compared with 41 per cent). If anything, the young women were slightly more likely to be studying for the most academic qualifications (34 per cent of those still in education studying for A levels compared with 32 per cent of the young men). This may simply reflect their overall better GCSE results.

Figure 5.2 shows the destinations at 16 for the main ethnic groups, reflecting a higher rate of staying on in education for ethnic minorities than for white respondents, confirming other recent reports (eg. Slade and Yates, 1993).

Although the overall rates of staying on were very high, some patterns began to emerge for those who did not continue studying. Those with the highest rates of staying on were those in the Chinese and Indian groups, the two groups which had the highest attainment at GCSE. However, all ethnic minorities had higher staying on rates than the white group. Going directly into training was highest in the Black Caribbean group, and lowest in the Chinese group. Going straight into a job was rare, but was most common for young white people.

Descriptions of non-educational initial destinations

A picture is thus emerging – the majority of the sample stayed on in full-time education, and those who did so were fairly equally spread across a range of studying locations such as their old school, or colleges of further education. For those, however, who responded that their initial destination was not full-time education, and who formed the small percentages who went into training (9 per cent), work (5 per cent) or something else (10 per cent), what specifically were they doing?

The group who started the year by enrolling on a YT training scheme were asked which type of training they were receiving. Results indicated that approximately half were being trained to do either office-type work (clerical and/or secretarial), technical-type work (including electrical engineering and mechanics) or caring. These occupational choices are very similar to those reported nationally by the Careers Service for 1992 leavers. Over four-fifths stated that they were working towards some kind of qualification.

YT can be based in a work environment, or at college, or can consist of a mixture of the two. Female trainees were more likely than male trainees to be doing most or all of their training in a work environment. Those trainees based entirely at a college or training centre were more likely than those on other types of schemes to have no qualifications at GCSE. Trainees based mainly in the workplace were most likely to be working towards a qualification (90 per cent).

Those who started the year in a job (5 per cent of the sample) were slightly more likely to be male than those who started the year in other ways (55 per cent). Most of the work being done seemed to be unskilled (for example labouring and production line), with approximately half of the sample in one of the following occupational categories: technical, hairdressing, catering/food, construction and manufacturing. The remainder were in retail, office work or doing something else. As a group, those who found a job were relatively unqualified: 5 per cent having five or more GCSEs at A-C grades, and a quarter having no qualifications at GCSE at all. Just under a third of employees in the sample were working towards a qualification of some sort.

Those who had found work were asked how they had got their jobs, and the answers to this question highlighted the importance of informal contacts, with 40 per cent having used connections and leads provided by family and friends. Newspaper advertisements were the second most frequent response, followed by the careers office, and through work experience or asking employers. The job centre and shop windows were reportedly the least useful options.

Of those whose initial destination was not one of these full-time options (one in ten of the sample), 60 per cent classified themselves as unemployed. Unemployment benefit for this age group was withdrawn in the 1988 social security benefits review, when 16-18 year olds became unable to claim financial support unless in exceptional circumstances, and so this classification does not represent an 'official' description. Many of the remainder of the group did not state what they were doing with their time, but some referred to part-time activities (study, training or work), waiting to start a full-time course, and caring or family commitments.

Destinations of those with no qualifications at GCSE

Those with more qualifications were, of course, more likely to stay on in education. The most interesting group to look at is those who did not get any GCSEs. The previous chapter showed that there were few in the sample without any qualifications at all, and in a group who were already selected on the basis of certain indices of disadvantage (such as area and ethnicity) this group are likely to be the most disadvantaged. The choices for them are extremely limited. What did they do first?

There were 272 young people without GCSEs. There was no over-representation of either gender in this group, just over half being young women (56 per cent) as in the full sample. There was, however, a slight over-representation of ethnic minorities, with more Black Caribbean, Bangladeshi, and Indian young people than in the full group of respondents, and fewer white people. Figure 5.3 shows their initial destinations in September 1993, ranked in order of the frequency with which they occurred. Study was still the most common option (39 per cent), although half as many followed this route than had in the full

Figure 5.3   Initial destinations of those with no qualifications at GCSE

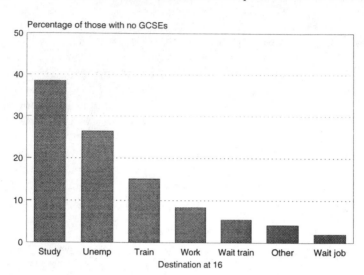

sample. Unemployment was the destination of a quarter (26 per cent) of the unqualified group, and the remainder were mostly either in training or waiting for training, with a small group (8 per cent) having found work. Even in this disadvantaged group, with no qualifications, staying on remained the most popular option.

Satisfaction with initial destination at age 16

The survey asked all respondents how happy they were with what they were doing. As Figure 5.4 shows, there was a marked difference between the levels of happiness reported by those with and without a full-time occupation. Less than 30 per cent of those *not* in full-time study, training or work stated that they were very or quite happy with what they were doing, compared with over three-quarters of those in full-time study, training or work.

There were few differences between the happiness of those doing different types of full-time occupation, although trainees were slightly less likely to be satisfied than those studying or those working.

Figure 5.4   Happiness with current occupation

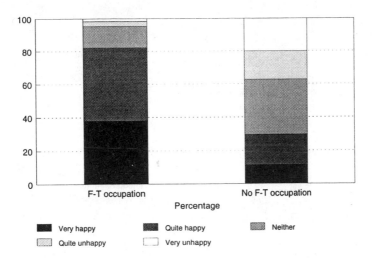

Percentage

- Very happy
- Quite happy
- Neither
- Quite unhappy
- Very unhappy

Conclusion

The rates of staying on in education were the most striking feature of this analysis of respondents' initial destinations. Small proportions started in full-time work or training. Despite a strong link between academic achievement and the likelihood of continuing in education, even within the small group who did not manage to achieve any GCSE results at all, staying on was still the most popular option. Having a full-time occupation meant that respondents were more likely to be satisfied with what they were doing.

6

A diary of the year

Did the people taking part in the *Changing Lives* survey continue with their initial occupation? How many of those studying completed a year of their chosen course, and how many dropped out and did something else? If they did not stay in education in the first instance, what did they do with their year?

Respondents' diaries, month by month

Merging the three waves of the *Changing Lives* survey provides us with information on activities during each month of a fifteen month period (from April 1993 to June 1994). For each month, respondents were asked to chose from one of four options describing their activities, including full-time study, full-time paid work, full-time training and none of these (eg, part-time work, unemployment, something else). Preliminary analyses (Shaw 1994c) suggested that the numbers in full-time education dropped between October 1993 and the summer of 1994, while those in full-time training or work remained fairly stable, and those in the 'None of these' category rose.

Access to the three waves allowed us to map the patterns more precisely. Figure 6.1 shows the pattern of activity for the whole sample from April 1993 to June 1994.

Between April and August 1993, the numbers stating that they were in full-time education dropped from over 80 per cent to 16 per cent, although there is clearly some scope for ambiguity in the interpretation of 'full-time education'. Some students had presumably already left school (or stopped attending) by April, others may have been on study leave. Some stated that they were in full-time education throughout the summer, perhaps re-sitting examinations or alternatively, for those who stayed on, simply regarding the transition from Year 11 to Year 12 as

Figure 6.1   Patterns of activity from April 1993 to June 1994

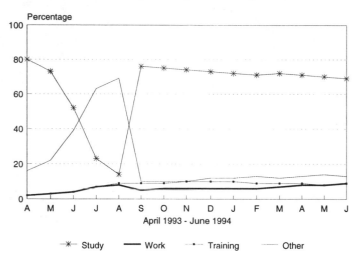

All waves

an unbroken period of study. Throughout this period the numbers in training and full-time work rose steadily, but always keeping a low absolute level. Neither exceed 11 per cent before August. In September, the numbers in full-time education reach their peak for the 1993-1994 academic session, at 79 per cent. From then they begin a steady decline to 70 per cent at the end of the academic year the following summer.

Meanwhile, training reaches a plateau at this point (August-September), and the proportions in full-time training remain at approximately 10 per cent for the remainder of the year. The numbers in full-time work drop at the start of the academic year, but gradually increase through until the following June. The increase in numbers in full-time work does not equal the drop in those in full-time education, however. Those doing something other than studying, working or training peak in the summer of 1993, but always remain higher than those in training or work.

Unless we concentrated on the group who responded to more than one questionnaire, we could not be sure that changes in the pattern throughout the year were not due to differences in the profiles of respondents to the second and third surveys. In order to examine the trends for the 'longitudinal' group only, who took part in at least two

Figure 6.2   Patterns of activity from March 1993 to June 1994 for the longitudinal sample only

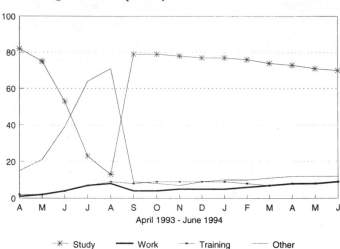

Longitudinal sample

waves, and for whom a continuous pattern can be mapped, Figure 6.2 presents the activities of this group alone.

As the attritional analyses had shown, the longitudinal sample were a slightly more successful and conformist group than the full sample. This was reflected in their year trends, as slightly more of them were in full-time education throughout the period than were the whole sample, shown in Figure 6.1 above. However, overall the patterns for the whole sample and for the longitudinal sample were very similar indeed, and we can assume that the patterns reflected real trends and were not an artefact of variations in respondents.

Identifying pathways through the year

Banks et al (1992) had identified five main 'career trajectories' in the ESRC 16-19 Initiative in the late 1980s, and these included:

1   Full-time education for at least two years (37 per cent).

2   One year post-compulsory education (12 per cent).

3   Through YTS into the labour market (25 per cent).

4   Education plus YTS, in any order (5 per cent).

5   Neither education nor YTS (21 per cent).

The *Changing Lives* sample faced a different situation in 1994, and, in addition, we had available a detailed diary for one year, rather than quarterly information over several years. Consequently, we defined a set of 'pathways' through the year for use with our sample, with the emphasis being on the amount of participation in full-time education, as this was the over-riding experience of sample members:

1   Study all year (73 per cent).

2   Study plus other: study first, then moving on to something else at some point later in the year (10 per cent), or something else first, but study at some point in the year (2 per cent).

3   Something other than studying all year (16 per cent).

Obviously, these analyses have to be based on the longitudinal sample only, as only they have the appropriate information from different parts of the year. It was possible to calculate a pathway for 1,601 of the 1,981 people in the longitudinal sample, and the remainder of this chapter is based on this group.

The next sections look more closely at each of these three pathways, and begin to untangle what each might mean for respondents.

Pathway 1: education all year

Figure 6.3 shows the month-by-month breakdown of the year for the 1,161 respondents (73 per cent) who took Pathway 1, full-time study. Obviously, from September onwards, they were all in education, but the first half of the figure shows that they were already more committed to education before they left full-time compulsory education in Year 11. Over 86 per cent were in full-time education in April 1993, compared with 80 per cent of the full sample (see Figure 6.2 above). By April 1994 some were beginning to leave full-time education, presumably having taken one year courses, and the last two months of the graph show a very small increase in the proportions in other activities.

These respondents, who had continued with full-time education for at least a year, were studying at a range of locations. Roughly one third

Figure 6.3   Month by month breakdown for respondents taking Pathway 1:
full-time education

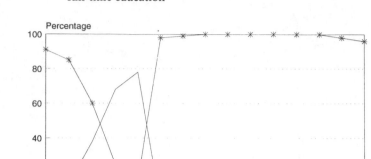

(35 per cent) had remained at the same school where they had received
their Year 11 education. A further third (32 per cent) had moved on to
a further education college, and a quarter (26 per cent) were at a sixth
form college. A very small proportion (5 per cent) had moved on to
another school, and the remainder (3 per cent) either did not answer
the question or were studying somewhere else. At the end of the year,
they were asked whether they were on a two year or one year course
of study. Of those still in full-time education at this point (95 per cent),
slightly more were on a two year course (58 per cent) rather than one
year (42 per cent). Very few were involved with work or training at any
point in the 15 month period from April 1993 to June 1994. At points
when they were not studying, for example in the Spring months of 1993
before Year 12 began, they were doing something else rather than
working or training.

Of those taking this 'studying' pathway, over a quarter (28 per cent)
were doing some GCSE re-sits, 15 per cent were taking new GCSE
subjects, 41 per cent were studying for GCE A levels and 3 per cent
were taking GCE A/S levels (these categories were not mutually exclusive). In terms of vocational, rather than academic, qualifications, just
under a quarter (23 per cent) were doing GNVQs, 21 per cent BTECs,

and 11 per cent NVQs. Half of all those on the studying path were doing some work experience as part of their courses (50 per cent).

Pathway 2: education, plus other activity during the year

Those who took the second path (187), involving at least one period of full-time education but also involving another activity during the year, were slightly more likely to have started off in September in colleges of further education (46 per cent) rather than in school (20 per cent at their old school, 3 per cent at a different school) or in sixth form colleges (20 per cent), suggesting that fewer than in representative samples were taking the traditional academic route, which usually involves staying on at the school where earlier qualifications have been achieved (Banks et al, 1992, Courtenay and McAleese, 1993). The numbers studying dropped steeply at the beginning of the academic year and fell from well over 90 per cent to 64 per cent two months later in November. To qualify for this pathway, students had to be on a full-time course for at least one month in the year. The majority of the group were, in fact, in full-time education at the start of the year (159) but a very small group (particularly considering the total sample for these analyses numbered 1,601) dipped back into education at a later stage (28). By the end of the year, less than one in five were still in full-time education, and of these, three quarters were on a two year course. Figure 6.4 shows their different activities through the year.

Questions concerning the type of course being followed were asked at the second wave, in February 1994, by which time most had left their courses. Information about what they were studying is thus limited to those who were still in education at this point. Numbers following this pathway were relatively small anyway, so caution must be exercised when generalising from these figures. At this point, in the Spring of 1994, those studying were following a variety of courses, and were fairly evenly spread across GCSE retakes, new GCSE subjects, A levels and vocational courses.

By the last months of the period, the proportions in other activities, including working and training, were rising month by month. Over a fifth of this group were in full-time work by the Spring of 1994 and so could, potentially, have been using initial study as a way to 'pass the time' while trying to find a job. Alternatively, some could have been resitting examinations at Christmas or in January (dates vary according to the different examining boards) and then have moved on to full-time

Figure 6.4   Month by month breakdown for respondents taking Pathway 2: education, plus another activity during the year

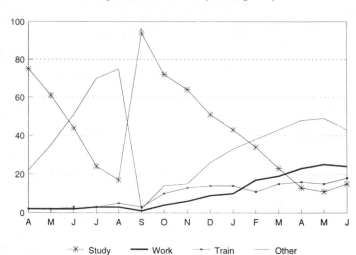

work having improved their Year 11 grades. A stable minority (approximately 15 per cent) were in full-time training from October onwards. The proportion without any full-time occupation stabilised at around 40 per cent towards the end of the year in question.

Those who do not start in education, but dip into it at some point during the year, are a very interesting but very small group, and numbers do not warrant separate analyses for them. We can only speculate that there might be several possible explanations for this interesting pattern. First, students may have found it hard to find a college at which to study, and were using training courses to 'fill in' until they could get onto courses. Second, they could have returned to college as a last resort after having unsuccessfully tried a range of other activities such as working and training.

Pathway 3: other all year

This pathway most closely resembles what Banks et al (1992) refer to as the 'traditional' transition. It includes everyone who left school at 16 and did not return within one year (254 people, 16 per cent of the longitudinal sample). What were they doing? Figure 6.5 presents their monthly breakdown.

Figure 6.5   Month by month breakdown for respondents taking Pathway 3:
activities other than education all year

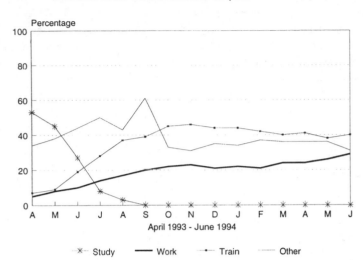

The patterns here were fairly consistent. Initial investment in education had been low with just over half in full-time education in April of
their last year of compulsory education. Throughout the year, between
one in five and one in four of this group were in full-time work, with
the proportion increasingly steadily throughout the year. The proportion on full-time training also increased steadily to begin with, reaching
a plateau at approximately 40 per cent, where it remained until the end
of the year. In any one month, between 30 and 60 per cent of the group
were engaged in 'other' activities, with this proportion peaking in
September and tailing off towards the end of the year. This category
includes unemployment. Respondents were only asked directly about
unemployment at three points – September, February and June. The
rates at each of these points were 25 per cent, 29 per cent and 29 per
cent (including those who said 'not sure' with those who said 'yes').

It would seem that many of those on this pathway were, thus, trying
to negotiate the employment market. At any one month, approximately
half were either in work or described themselves as being unemployed;
more may have been engaged in 'stalling' activities which might hide
underlying unemployment.

Part-time work

The first and third questionnaires both included questions about part-time work. These did not form part of the occupation diary, but provided snapshot information in September and June. At the start of the academic year, 20 per cent of the *Changing Lives* sample had a part-time job and a further 33 per cent were looking for part-time work. By June the percentage working part-time had risen to 24 per cent. Full-time students were most likely to engage in part-time employment, the proportion doing so rising from 23 per cent to 29 per cent over the academic year. Those following Pathway 3 were least likely to engage in part-time work, around one in ten doing so in both September and June, suggesting that part-time work is not 'masking' unemployment to any great extent.

Conclusion

Confirming all previous reports of recent trends, the majority of the *Changing Lives* sample stayed on in education after the end of Year 11. A larger proportion stayed on than had been reported in any previous study. Given the nature of the sample and our confidence that they were fairly representative of young people at inner-city, mixed-ethnicity schools, we conclude that this reflects a continuing trend for rising numbers to remain in education, rather than anything particular to this group. However, the interesting point is that, despite the fact that the *Changing Lives* sample members were significantly disadvantaged in terms of their Year 11 academic attainments – if compared with national examination results – similar proportions were staying on in full-time education as were in the national Careers Service figures for the same year. This would seem to support Payne's (1995a) conclusion that the staying-on rates are increasing most in those at the bottom of the academic achievement continuum.

Preliminary analysis of three main pathways taken by respondents revealed much heterogeneity in the patterns for those who had *not* taken the full-time education route. The next chapter looks at the distinguishing features of those taking the various pathways.

7

Predicting different pathways

Three main pathways through the first year post-compulsory education were identified in the last chapter, indicating either (1) full-time education throughout the year, (2) education plus other activities or (3) activities excluding education. Simply outlining the pathways taken by the cohort has already indicated some variations among those following the different routes. As would be expected, it seems that some are more likely to follow certain pathways than are others. For example, only half as many of those on Pathway 3 had been in full-time education in April 1993 as those who followed Pathway 1. Those who were going to be taking the least academic pathway were thus opting out of their full-time education at the earliest opportunity.

In this chapter, we move on to look in more detail at who takes which pathway in the hope of identifying some predictive factors that may be of use to schools and careers services. We began by exploring whether the proportions taking each pathway varied by gender, ethnicity, qualifications or the area that the school was in.

Pathways by gender, ethnicity, GCSE results and school area

Despite the fact that gender was significantly related to GCSE results, young women, who as a group performed better than the young men, were no more likely than the young men to follow the 'education' pathway (75 per cent compared with 74 per cent respectively), nor any more likely to follow any other pathway. This is particularly interesting in the case of the final pathway, where respondents were engaged in activities other than education all year, as we had joined Banks et al (1992) in identifying this as the 'traditional' pathway. As such, we might have expected it to apply more to young men than young women. However, 16 per cent of both sexes took this route. Others have

Figure 7.1   Pathways through the year, by ethnic group

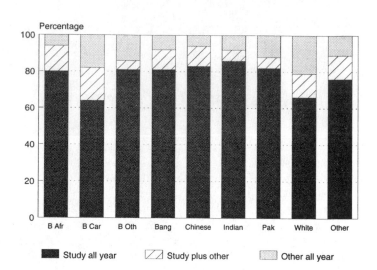

suggested that the differences between the trajectories followed by young men and young women begin to emerge after leaving compulsory education, but we find no support for this argument in terms of the pathways taken in this cohort of inner city young people.

Did the pathway taken vary by ethnicity? Figure 7.1 presents the different patterns for each of the ethnic groups.

These bars confirm the diversity of experience for each of the ethnic groups. It is interesting to note the apparent similarity of the Black Caribbean group to the white group. Both these groups have lower proportions following the education trajectory than the others, and larger proportions following the 'Other all year' trajectory.

One of the main findings from Banks et al (1992) was the very big effect of educational attainment on career trajectory taken. The *Changing Lives* sample had a rather different educational profile and different options than those that were open to the 16-19 Initiative cohorts, but Figure 7.2 shows that this very strong relationship was replicated in our longitudinal sample.

Of those with the best GCSE results, nearly all continued to study. Of those with no GCSEs, under 20 per cent followed the studying pathway throughout the year. The fact that any did at all is very interesting, suggesting either that education has taken on a new role of

Figure 7.2   Pathways through the year, by Year 11 academic attainment

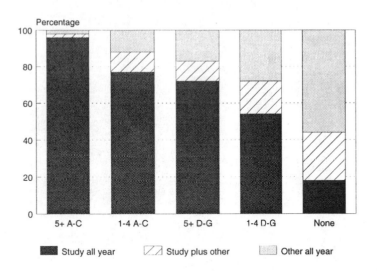

'holding' disadvantaged students in the absence of other occupational options, or that those without qualifications are increasingly being encouraged to stay on. The introduction of NVQs and GNVQs in colleges and some sixth forms has increased the availability of foundation level vocational courses aimed at those with low academic qualifications.

As we progress down the GCSE attainment continuum, increasing proportions of respondents fall into the pathway mixing education with other activities. These people may be remaining in education until other options become open to them, or they may be simply dropping out of education without anything else to go to. Virtually all of those who started the year doing something other than studying, but came to it at some point in the year, fall into the bottom group of those with no academic qualifications. Finally, the proportions doing something else all year also increase down the continuum, with over half of the group without qualifications being in this situation. As we know that only a very small minority of the unqualified (6 per cent by March) are actually in full-time work, we will need to explore what these people are doing.

In addition, the proportions taking each of the pathways varied depending on the area that their school was based in. These patterns are shown in Figure 7.3.

Figure 7.3   Pathways through the year, by TEC area

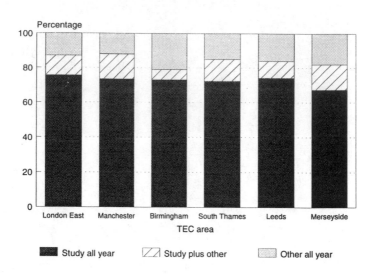

Once again, it is difficult to interpret the area differences, as the young people were not drawn from school catchment areas which directly match the TEC areas, and they were not representative of school leavers in the TEC areas as a whole. However, the effect of local careers opportunities is obviously an important factor in the pathways followed on leaving compulsory education.

Predicting pathways: multivariate statistical analyses

A picture is beginning to emerge, indicating that those who are most disadvantaged in terms of their academic qualifications and area factors are tending to take the non-education routes, perhaps as a matter of drift rather than a matter of choice. In order to determine whether any of the background factors, such as gender, ethnicity, examination record and school variables, have an independent effect on the choice of pathway taken, this next section introduces multivariate statistical analyses. In multivariate analyses, the outcome variable (eg. choice of Pathway 1) is termed the *dependent variable*, and the predicting factors (eg. qualifications) are the *independent variables*.

The process used is called logistic regression. Similar to a multiple regression technique, logistic regression is used to predict a dichotomous variable (an 'either/or' outcome) rather than a continuous variable (ranging from a very low score to a very high score). Thus, it is particularly appropriate in these circumstances when we do not want to rank the pathways taken, but simply want to distinguish between those who did, or did not, take any given route. The version used was that to be found in a statistical software package for the social sciences called SPSS (version 6.1 for Windows). For a fuller presentation of technical aspects of the analysis, see Appendix 3.

It is, however, worth introducing a word of caution at this stage, for two main reasons. The first is that there are arguments for and against running multivariate analyses on weighted data. Secondly, given the rather specific and unique nature of the sample, we need to be careful about drawing broader conclusions from these results. Together with the fact that the sampling of sets of schools in different areas might affect error terms in the models, it is important to view these analyses as initial and exploratory, requiring replication and further research for confirmation.

A set of three models was run to predict the probability of students taking each of the three main pathways. Thus, the first model sought to predict which respondents took the educational pathway, the second whether they took an 'education plus other' pathway, and the third to predict whether they would take the 'traditional' pathway. Each model investigated which factors were the most important in predicting the route taken. Thus, for example, did ethnic origin predict whether they took Pathway 1 or not?

Two types of factors were used in the analyses as potential predictors of route taken. The first were continuous variables, such as academic achievement. The second were categorical variables, such as which type of school had been attended. The variables are summarised and presented in Table 7.1.

The variables were entered into the equation in order of statistical significance. That is, the variables that contributed the most to predicting whether a Year 11 student took any given route were entered first. Other variables were then entered in descending order of significance until only non-significant predictors were excluded. At each stage, the significance of a variable in contributing to the prediction was assessed once all the factors already in the equation were held constant.

Each model had three main stages, each reflecting a 'layer' of analysis. In the first stage, the contribution of background variables was assessed. In a sense, these are best considered as those factors which the

Table 7.1   Variables included in the multivariate analyses

Variable type	Number	Label	Description
Continuous	1	GCSEs	Year 11 academic qualification score
	2	Truant	Truancy in years 10 and 11
	3	Likesch	Attitude to school scale
Categorical	4	Gender	Whether female or not
	5	Black	From a black ethnic origin group or not
	6	Asian	From an Asian ethnic origin group or not
	7	Skilled	Parent in skilled manual work
	8	Nonman	Parent in non-manual work
	9	Notwork	Head of household not working
	10	School	School type: Grant maintained or voluntary aided
	11	Sixth	Whether the school had a sixth form
	12	League	Whether the school was in the top third of the local league table
	13	TEC	TEC area in which the school was situated

Reference groups for categorical variables
Gender = male; Black = not Black; Asian = not Asian; Skilled = unskilled or professional parent; Nonman = parent in manual work; Notwork = head of household in paid work; School = county school; Sixth = school having no sixth form; League = school in bottom two-thirds of table; TEC = TEC area 1

individuals would have brought to school with them, including their gender, their ethnicity and the socio-economic status of their parents' occupation. In the second stage, a layer of school factors was added, those that would have had their effect, or been accumulated, during the school years, including academic attainment, level of truanting in the last two years, whether the school was grant maintained or voluntary aided, whether the school had a sixth form, and where the school was placed in the local league table. Finally, the last layer included TEC area, as this was what was faced when the individual considered leaving the school and entering the world of work or training. At each stage, only the significant variables from the previous stage were retained.

Table 7.2   The influence of various factors on the probability of taking each of the main post-compulsory education pathways

Model Variable	Result
Model 1: Took Pathway 1, full-time education	
Asian	Prob. increased, compared with non-Asian
Skilled	Prob. decreased if from a skilled background
GCSEs	Prob. increased with better GCSEs
Likesch	Prob. increased if had liked school
League	Prob. increased if a high-league school
Truancy	Prob. decreased if had skipped school
TEC	Prob. varied by TEC area
Model 2: Took Pathway 2, education plus other activities	
Asian	Prob. decreased, compared with non-Asian
GCSEs	Prob. decreased with better GCSEs
Truancy	Prob. increased if had skipped school
Model 3: Took Pathway 3, other activities all year	
Gender	Prob. increased if female
Asian	Prob. decreased compared with non-Asian
Black	Prob. decreased compared with non-Black
Skilled	Prob. increased if from skilled background
GCSEs	Prob. decreased with higher GCSEs
Likesch	Prob. decreased if had liked school
League	Prob. decreased if a high-league school
Truancy	Prob. increased if had skipped school
TEC	Prob. varied by TEC area.

Table 7.2 presents a summary of the significant variables indicated in each of the final models. Full details of the results from the analyses can be found in Appendix 3.

The important thing to remember when assessing the final models is that the results for each variable are so when *all the other factors in the model are held constant*. Thus, in the first model, the increased probability of those from Asian groups staying on at school is so even after controlling for their better GCSE results.

Not surprisingly, those who took the continuing education pathway were those who had liked school, had done well at school, and who had attended a school which was well placed in its local league table. They were less likely to be from skilled backgrounds, and this may reflect parental attitudes or identification with parents on the part of the student. They were also more likely to be from one of the four Asian groups, which included Bangladeshi, Chinese, Indian and Pakistani families. Numbers were too small to allow any further breakdown of this category. They were not less likely to be from one of the Black groups, and any differences we had seen emerging earlier between Black ethnicities and others disappeared after controlling for other variables including GCSEs.

Those taking the second pathway, involving some education but also other activities, formed a small and heterogeneous group, and this is reflected in the fact that few factors emerged as significant predictors. In this case, having lower GCSEs was a predictor, as was having been a truanter at school. Asian students were less likely to take this path than either white or black students.

Those on the third 'traditional' pathway, leaving school at 16 and becoming involved in the labour market (either through employment, training or unemployment) were more likely to be female, white, from skilled backgrounds, and with a range of negative school attributes including a dislike of school, lower GCSEs, and higher truancy. Those from ethnic minorities were not likely to take this pathway.

The TEC area of the school was important in determining whether the education pathway or the traditional pathway was taken. It did not feature as a predictive factor for those who took the more nebulous and varied pathways in and out of education. At this stage, we can but note this, and suggest that area factors *are* important in lives after compulsory education, even after controlling for differing types of schools and examination results. However, determining exactly what it is about the TECs that plays a role is beyond the power of these data. Each of the areas has unique demographic, labour market, education and training policy features which would need further exploration in order to identify what it is about different areas that influences pathways taken.

There are several main points to note from these results. First, even at the disadvantaged end of the aged 16 population, GCSE results are of paramount importance in predicting which pathway will be followed. Less than a quarter of the *Changing Lives* sample achieved five or more A-C grades, the types of grades most usually associated with staying on in full-time education, yet their grades retained a universal and significant predictive value in analysing their pathways in Year 12.

Second, it seems that in areas of inner-city deprivation, the differences between black groups and white groups begin to fade once other factors on which they might vary are taken into account. Thus, black and white groups were equally likely to stay on at school once background, school and area factors were taken into account, although Asian respondents were more likely to do so. It should be remembered that this was a particularly selected group of white young people. Whilst the majority of Britain's ethnic minority population continues to live in inner urban areas, the same cannot be said of the white population. We are, thus, comparing the black groups with a non-representative white group who are more disadvantaged than most white groups.

The one place where the white group stood out was in the increased likelihood that white respondents would follow the third, more traditional pathway. It is not clear whether this is a particularly advantageous way to go, but is more of an option for the white group than for others from ethnic minorities. It might be that this trajectory is associated with traditional, inner-city skilled-manual cultures, where work or activity of some kind is provided by other family members or friends rather than through careers services, or where there is a family history of labouring in certain industries. Alternatively, there may be stronger discriminatory practices at work in the local labour markets than there are in the local colleges and on training courses. Finally, a quarter of this group were unemployed on the three occasions when the question was asked, and the differences between ethnic groups might reflect differences in educational aspirations, with the unqualified in some groups heading for the employment market rather than aspiring to stay on at school.

Young women were slightly more likely than young men to follow this third, non-educational, route. The reasons for this were not clear. It might have been that family commitments were making full-time education difficult, but more data are needed to untangle this finding.

The next section goes on to look in more detail at the factors predicting entry into the labour market for those who spend at least part of the year working.

Factors predicting entry into the labour market

The final, 'traditional' pathway included those who had been involved in training all year, or in 'other' activities all year, as well as those who had dipped in and out of full-time employment. This pathway excluded young people who had spent any time in full-time education during the year. Pathway 2, on the other hand, did include some respondents who

Table 7.3   Factors associated with finding any full-time work

Variable	Relationship
Asian	Prob. decreased compared with non-Asian
Black	Prob. decreased compared with non-Black
GCSEs	Prob. decreased with better GCSE results
Truancy	Prob. increased if skipped school
Likesch	Prob. decreased if had liked school
TEC	Prob. varied by TEC area

had worked at some point during the year. In order to explore in more detail the factors particularly involved in finding full-time work during the year after school, a new variable was created. This indicated whether or not an individual had spent any month since September 1993 in full-time work. A total of 21 per cent (416) of the longitudinal sample had done so.

Earlier preliminary and cross-sectional analyses (Shaw, 1994a) had already suggested that those in full-time work at the beginning of the year were likely to be relatively unqualified, and less than a third were working towards a qualification of any sort. Forty per cent had been able to use connections and leads provided by family and friends when finding employment. To explore factors having a predictive value, we ran further logistic regression analyses. Table 7.3 presents a summary of the results, with 'any work' as a dependent variable.

We found that, as with predicting who would follow Pathway 3, those who had been in full-time employment at any time in the year following the end of compulsory education were more likely to be white, to have done less well at school, and to be in certain TEC areas. Some of these results were echoed in the comments of sample members written on their questionnaires. One wrote, 'I would like to say, for young Asians it is very difficult to find any jobs, no matter their qualifications'. Similarly, another commented, 'Asian people don't get good jobs because of prejudice against our colour. Even if two people have good qualifications and the Asian person had better qualifications than the other, then the other would get the job'. A third wrote, 'I have been looking for a part-time job since last summer holiday and I couldn't find one, I don't know why – is it my colour or what? You tell me!' The answer is a composite of factors in which ethnicity plays a part.

Factors predicting any experience of training during the year

Similarly, young people following either Pathway 2 or 3 might have spent at least a short length of time in training. The previous analyses had already suggested that people following these pathways were those who had not done as well at school, and also that ethnicity played a (varying) part. We decided to take a closer look at the issue of full-time YT for the *Changing Lives* sample.

In recent years, the proportion of young people in training has dropped as staying on in education has grown more popular. A number of initiatives have been introduced in order to persuade young people that they should be making an active contribution to their training, rather than seeing it as something which just happens to them when they have nothing else to do. One of these initiatives was the introduction of pilot 'training credits' schemes in 1990. This involved an entitlement to train to approved standards for 16 and 17 year olds who had left full-time education. Each credit displayed a monetary value and gave access to an individual training account. These are exchanged for training with an employer or training provider. Early indications suggested that take-up of training credits was lower than expected, that students' knowledge and understanding of them is uneven, but that some TECs have been relatively successful in disseminating information about the scheme (HMI, 1992). Three of the TEC areas under study were running pilot training credit schemes: Merseyside, Birmingham and South Thames. *Changing Lives* 3 reported that at least half of all trainees had some awareness of the system, and that this was strongest in Birmingham where the scheme had been running for the longest period.

In relation to training schemes more generally, evidence has suggested that, at least in terms of take-up, young people from ethnic minorities were benefiting from schemes (Stares et al, 1982), although this was almost certainly offset by the finding that ethnic minority young people tended to find themselves allocated to schemes with relatively poor job prospects (Cross and Smith, 1987).

As Chapter 5 reported, over half of trainees were being trained to do either office type work (clerical and/or secretarial), technical-type work (including electrical, engineering and mechanics) or caring. The female trainees were more likely to be doing most or all of their training in a work environment. Over four-fifths of trainees stated that they were working towards some kind of qualification. Trainees who had not done particularly well at school were more likely to be doing their training at a college or training centre, whereas those with better GCSEs had gone into workplace-based training.

Earlier, preliminary analyses had reported that, by February 1994, the young women in the sample were particularly likely to be training for a traditionally female occupation and very unlikely to enter or train for a traditionally male job (Shaw, 1994b). While young men were somewhat more inclined to enter traditionally male areas of employment, the distinction was less marked. Such gender stereotyping was more extreme among those on YT than those in employment. Answers to questions in the third wave suggested that this gender stereotyping had been, at least in part, a conscious choice on the part of trainees. Over three-quarters reported that they were being trained for the kind of work they wanted, 13 per cent had not known what they wanted, and fewer than one in ten were training for a job they had not wanted.

Less than 10 per cent of the *Changing Lives* sample were involved in full-time training (YT) at the beginning of the year, and this figure remained constant throughout. This was not necessarily the same group throughout, and some respondents had dipped in and out of training at some point – though less than had experimented with full-time work. Overall, 18 per cent of the longitudinal sample had spent at least one month in training during the year. Only 7 per cent reported full-time training for six months or more of the year, and only 1 per cent reported full-time training for 12 months. From these data, we constructed another new variable indicating whether or not the respondent had spent at least one month in training after leaving full-time compulsory education.

To explore some of the factors that might be relevant in determining who participated in training, a further set of logistic regressions were run, with any training as the dependent variable. Once again, a three stage approach was taken, where background variables, school based variables, and TEC area were entered progressively, retaining the significant variables from the previous stage in each new stage. Table 7.4 presents the results of the final model.

Young people from black ethnic groups were more likely than those from other ethnicities to spend part of their year in full-time training. As with those who found some work, a dislike of school, truancy and lower GCSE scores were predictive factors. It is interesting to note that those from families where the head of household was not in work were more likely to go into training than those from other backgrounds, suggesting that the need to bring in some income (however small) to

Table 7.4   Factors associated with doing any full-time training

Variable	Relationship
Asian	Prob. decreased compared with non-Asian
Black	Prob. increased compared with non-Black
Skilled	Prob. increased with skilled background
Notwork	Prob. increased if head of household not working
GCSEs	Prob. decreased with better GCSE results
Truancy	Prob. increased if skipped school
Likesch	Prob. decreased if had liked school
Sixth	Prob. decreased if the school had a sixth form
TEC	Prob. varied by TEC area

the family budget may be a motivating factor. It is also noteworthy that training is the only outcome where the type of school attended is a factor. Those having attended a school with a sixth form until Year 11 were less likely subsequently to spend any time in training.

We have already seen that, in the *Changing Lives* sample, the Asian respondents were more likely than other ethnicities to stay on in full-time education. We have also seen that those from the white group were more likely than the others to have found at least one month of full-time work. Here we found that those from the black ethnic minorities were more likely than the other groups to have done at least one month of YT. By concentrating too much on these results there is a danger of oversimplifying the story, because – despite the fact that as a group they were more likely than black or white respondents to be in full-time education – *some* Asian respondents will have done YT. Similarly, despite the fact that, as a group, they were less likely than the Asian respondents to stay on at school, it was still the case that *most* white and black respondents remained in full-time education. Only one in five of the whole group found one month or more of work or training. However, it does seem that there are some pathways and options that are more likely to be followed by some groups rather than others.

By the end of the year – final destinations

So far in this chapter we have looked at patterns of activity during the year. It seems appropriate to close with a snapshot of respondents' activities at the time of the final questionnaire in June 1994. Obviously, given the large numbers who had opted to take the 'education all year' pathway, plus those who had dipped in and out of education, the majority of those answering the third questionnaire (2,430) were still studying, a total of 68 per cent (1,662). Fifty-eight per cent of these were on a two year course at this point, the others on a one year course. Approximately similar proportions were working (9 per cent), in full-time training (9 per cent) or classified themselves as unemployed (10 per cent). The remaining 3 per cent were doing something else.

Conclusion

Following a course of full-time education, is an option taken by many inner-city young people when they leave compulsory education. Whether or not they chose this pathway depended in part on whether their GCSEs were sufficient, and how they got on at school in general. Two other main factors influence which pathway is taken. The first is ethnicity, in that Asian students were more likely to stay on in education. There were no differences between white and black groups in this respect. The second is the TEC area in which their school was based. In some TECs, more chose this pathway than in others.

However, exploring who takes the pathway that does not include education indicates different factors at work. Here it is the white inner city young people who chose, or were forced down, the labour market route and who managed to find at least one month of full-time work. Those from other groups of ethnic minorities, black and Asian, were less likely to take this course. Once again, this was more likely to be an option for those who had done less well at school, and more likely in some TEC areas than others. The possibility that local discrimination was in operation is suggested by the fact that many of those who had found work had done so through family and friends. Finally, doing at least one month of training was more likely for black respondents than for those from other ethnic groups, and for those who come from a household whose head was not in work.

It is worth highlighting again the fact that gender appears to have little role in predicting the pathway a young person will take at 16, despite the significant differences in attainment at GCSE between girls and boys. The only exception to this was that young women were more likely than young men to opt out of education entirely and follow the third route which did not involve any study.

8

Experiences, attitudes and aspirations

In all three waves of *Changing Lives*, the respondents' own perceptions of their experiences, attitudes and aspirations over the year were recorded. Overall, the preliminary reports had suggested that many of the young people questioned were satisfied with the situations they found themselves in, although some were finding aspects of their lives difficult to negotiate. This chapter looks in more detail at variations in their experiences as reported during the year of the study.

Happiness with path followed

In Chapter 5, we looked at respondents' satisfaction with their initial destination. Respondents were also asked about their happiness with their situation at each of the subsequent two waves of data collection, allowing us to see whether their satisfaction changed during the year. Table 8.1 presents the average levels of their happiness, broken down by gender, for the longitudinal sample. This was originally rated on a five point scale from 1 (very happy) to 5 (very unhappy) but for clarity of presentation we have reversed this so that a high score indicated higher levels of happiness.

Table 8.1   Average levels of happiness throughout the year

Gender	Average happiness September 1993	Average happiness February 1994	Average happiness June 1994
Female	4.05	3.82	3.88
Male	3.99	3.76	3.80
Weighted base	*1,899*	*1,606*	*1,959*

Table 8.2   Average levels of happiness, by pathway taken, June 1994

Pathway		Weighted number of respondents*	Average happiness
1	Study all year	1,156	3.97
2	Study plus other	185	3.51
3	Other all year	250	3.68

(p<.001)
* Some respondents did not answer the question

At all times, the young women reported slightly higher levels of happiness with what they were doing than the young men, but the difference was not statistically significant.

Levels of happiness by the end of the year did vary, however, according to which of the three main pathways had been followed by that point. To recount, the pathways identified were (1) Study all year, (2) Study plus other activities, and (3) Other activities all year. Table 8.2 presents the average levels of happiness with the routes taken, broken down by pathway.

Those in full-time education were the most satisfied by the end of the year, and those who had done some studying but also did something else during the year were the least satisfied. Those who had done other activities all year, fell in between these two extremes. This again suggests that, at least for some young people, staying on in education for part of the year (while also engaging in some other activities such as training) is a holding operation, not a positive choice. Had it been a positive choice, presumably they would have been happier with it.

We also compared levels of happiness by whether or not respondents fell into the group who had done at least one month of full-time work, or into the group who had done at least one month of full-time training. Both these comparisons were non-significant, and the average levels of satisfaction with what respondents were doing by the end of the year did not vary.

Experiences of staying on in education all year

As we have seen, the majority of the sample were in some kind of full-time education throughout the year, and the 'Study all year' pathway was the overwhelming choice of most respondents. The three waves of data collection provided a wealth of information about how these students made the choice to stay in education, and how they were coping.

At the start of the year, respondents were asked about the ways in which they had got advice about what to do at the end of Year 11. We have already seen that, overall, formal Careers Service information had been found to be useful, more so than in-school services, and that advice from families and friends was also valued. Those who followed the education pathway throughout the year, in fact found advice from parents and teachers to be the most helpful sources of information (31 per cent in each case stating it to be 'very helpful'), closely followed by an interview with the careers officer (30 per cent). Careers lessons in school were less likely to be rated as being 'very helpful' (19 per cent) by this group, perhaps because of their more general content. These findings might reflect the fact that those who are setting off on an educational pathway will already have better contacts within their schools and be more likely to chat to their teachers than those who go on other activities. Subject teachers would in addition be expected to be able to provide detailed information about further study in their particular field. Furthermore, those who follow a more exclusively educational pathway are more likely to come from homes where the general level of parental education is higher (15 per cent of fathers with a degree, compared to 4 per cent of those on other pathways), and this might lead to more encouragement to continue with education from the home front as well.

In the second wave of questionnaires respondents were asked to say how easy they were finding the studying. Those who remained in education all year were likely to have found the studying easier or about the same as they had anticipated – 10 per cent and 55 per cent respectively. A substantial minority (35 per cent) however, had found their courses harder than they had expected, and we might hypothesise that these could have been young people who, in different historical contexts, might not have stayed on in education at all. Those who continued with their study throughout the year were also likely to be those who were still feeling up-to-date with the course by February (63 per cent). A third (34 per cent) had felt a bit behind and 4 per cent had felt very behind at that stage. As a group, they had been reasonably good attenders when questioned in February, with nearly half always attending classes (49 per cent), and the majority of the remainder only missing occasional classes (42 per cent). Only 6 per cent occasionally missed days, and the remaining 3 per cent missed more or hardly ever attended. The multivariate analyses had suggested that this group had been among the better attenders at school in the first place, so the fact that they continued to be so is not particularly surprising.

Why had they decided to stay on in full-time education in the first place? At the end of the year, those still in education were asked to indicate their reasons for staying on from a list of possibilities. Respondents could indicate as many reasons as they wished. Table 8.3 presents the stated reasons for remaining in education, in descending order of frequency.

Table 8.3   Reasons for remaining in full-time education

Reason	Per cent
I wanted to improve my qualifications	53
I want to go to university eventually	49
I need more qualifications for the job I want	44
I was really interested in the subject(s) I've been studying	25
My family wanted me to	20
It's better than being unemployed	17
That's what most of my friends were doing	8
I didn't know what else to do	8
I couldn't find a job	6
Other reason	2

Weighted base, longitudinal sample, Pathway 1 n=1,161

Qualification related reasons were obviously top of the list with over half of the sample wanting to improve their qualifications (53 per cent), many with the intention of trying for university. Social pressures, from family and friends, were lower in the hierarchy, as were reasons to do with not having any other option or preferring this to unemployment. Thus, despite the fact that levels of uptake of *advice* from families had been reported to be high, this was not associated with very high levels of family *pressure*. In addition, it is possible that pressure from family relates, in part at least, to not having other options. Although the proportions stating lack of other options as a reason for staying on are small, it is still worth noting that nearly one in five (17 per cent) stated that they continued with education because it was preferable to unemployment.

As we stated in *Changing Lives 3,* reports from the YCS suggested that staying-on rates bore little relation to local labour market conditions, but in our longitudinal analyses we have found that pathways taken are related at least in part to some features of the local area, although we were unable to untangle whether these were to do with labour market characteristics or not. There is enough evidence in our results to suggest that local conditions, and perhaps personal perceptions of these (which might vary from the reality) are having some kind of effect. For example, students may feel that they have no other option and so choose to study rather than be unemployed, even though their chances might not be as depressed as they expect. This might particularly be the case with ethnic minorities if, as Penn and Scattergood (1992) reported, they were less likely to even *try* to find work than their white peers.

At the end of the year, respondents were asked to look back and consider whether they had made the right decision. In *Changing Lives 3,* cross-sectional analyses suggested that those in education at the time of the last wave were most likely to have been satisfied, on reflection, with their initial choices. Looking within the longitudinal sample, at those who had been in education all year, this pattern is confirmed. Nearly three-quarters (73 per cent) felt that they had made the right decision. Only 8 per cent felt it had been a wrong decision and the remainder were either unsure (15 per cent) or felt that they had had no choice (4 per cent).

Experiences of pathways other than full-time education all year

The remainder of the sample either combined education with other activities (including unemployment) or had done other activities all year (total of 439). Not everyone had provided information about careers advice in the first wave. These limited data suggested that these two groups' experiences of their year were similar and, for this reason and because the numbers are fairly small, they are analysed together in this section. Some initial comparisons of the experiences of these people can be made with those taking the full-time education pathway.

It appeared that this group of those who combined education with other activities or did other activities all year were less likely to have reported that they found careers advice from their parents helpful (overall 29 per cent compared to 41 per cent of those on the full-time education pathway), and less likely to have felt that their school teachers had been very helpful (32 per cent compared to 42 per cent). However, they were slightly more likely to find school-based careers lessons very helpful (31 per cent compared to 26 per cent). This pattern of results suggests that for these routes, specialist careers advice and lessons were helpful, but more informal advice sources were used less. Given that the choices available to young people going into training and non-educational activities have been changing rapidly over recent years, this might be a reflection of the knowledge base of general teachers and parents, who may feel more confident talking to young people who are likely to follow the full-time education route.

Over half (60 per cent) of those following the routes involving activities other than education reported changes in what they were doing between September and January, and rather fewer (35 per cent) between January and June. Exploring the reasons for changes in activities revealed that these were most frequently attributed to not being happy with their previous activity (a third in both cases) or to money problems (23 per cent in January, 34 per cent in June). Problems with satisfaction with the activity chosen were sometimes referred to by respondents in the open-ended section of the questionnaires. Thus, one wrote, 'Tutors put me off the course, they acted as if I was supposed to know everything. I was the only school-leaver there, all the others were nearly onto 18 +. Very unfriendly, tutors unhelpful. [This was the] reason why I left after three weeks.' This might be partly a lack of preparation, and a lack of knowledge about what to expect from different options.

This group of respondents, which included those who had spent some time in full-time education as well as those who had done activities other than education all year, generally felt more dissatisfied with their Year 11 decision than those who stayed in full-time education throughout the year. Thirty per cent believed that, on reflection, they had made the wrong decision, and a further quarter (24 per cent) were not sure. Forty-two per cent felt that they had made the right decision and 5 per cent felt that they had had no choice.

Finally, if we compared only those who stuck to the full-time education pathway with those who dropped out of education during the year to do other activities, could we spot any correlates of dropping out? We isolated a group who had started off in education at the beginning of the year but did not complete a full year (159 young people). These people were more likely to have started their studies at further education colleges than those who stayed in full-time education all year (50 per cent compared with 32 per cent), and to have found their classes harder than expected (41 per cent compared with 35 per cent), and over half (56 per cent) reported that they were a bit or very behind with their studying half way through the year. In fact, by this stage, over a third (36 per cent) admitted to hardly ever attending classes. It seems unlikely, from these results, that they moved on from education as a positive step, but rather that they were not coping with their classes and were thus forced to try another activity instead.

Attitudes to employment and training

At each stage of the data collection, respondents' views were canvassed on various issues relating to employment, training, and other topics. In relation to the set of seven attitudinal questions in the first wave on attitudes to work, training and unemployment, *Changing Lives 1* reported that a positive attitude to training was shown in general, but attitudes to YT – in particular whether it constituted 'slave labour' – were ambivalent with roughly equal numbers agreeing, disagreeing and being unsure. Confirming some of these negative impressions, one respondent wrote, 'YT ... a waste of time (except the money) – no one should be led into it!' Responses to questions about unemployment showed that it was not regarded as being a desirable alternative to work, however unsatisfactory the work might be. Overall, respondents did not agree that it was essential to have a job to participate in society or to get satisfaction out of life. There were some ethnic group differences in response patterns, with Asian groups being more likely than others to agree that having a job was important to satisfaction with life.

In Table 8.4 we show the responses to these attitudinal questions of those who ended up following each of the three main pathways through the year.

Interesting differences emerge. Those in full-time education were slightly less attached to the idea that a job was necessary to feel part of society, and were more likely to believe that satisfaction could be achieved without working. Those who were likely to have had at least some experience of training were more negative about it than those who had not experienced it: 40 and 38 per cent versus 28 per cent believing it to be slave labour, and 67 and 59 per cent believing it better to have training before a job compared with 76 per cent. Those trying

Table 8.4   Attitudes, by pathways

Per cent agree/strongly agree

	Pathway 1 education	Pathway 2 educ. &other	Pathway 3 other all year
A person must have a job to feel a full member of society	23	25	28
It is much better to get some kind of training than to go straight into a paid job	76	67	59
Having almost any job is better than being unemployed	54	64	69
Youth training schemes are just slave labour	28	40	38
Once you've got a job, it's important to hang on to it even if you don't really like it	27	38	42
If I didn't like a job I'd pack it in, even if there was no other job to go to	20	24	25
A person can get satisfaction out of life without having a job	42	38	35

Weighted samples , numbers vary by question

to get into the employment market were more likely to believe that holding on to a job, once found, was very important (42 per cent and 38 per cent versus 27 per cent).

In the second wave, further attitudinal questions were asked, those relating to the use and relevance of school experiences having already been reported in Chapter 4. Responses to two additional statements concerning finding work are presented in Table 8.5.

Despite the fact that the differences between groups look very slight here, these differences were nevertheless statistically significant. Those following the full-time education pathway were, interestingly, more sympathetic to the cause of unemployed young people, disagreeing that their unemployment was attributable to lack of effort. This group were also more confident about their job prospects, disagreeing with the

Table 8.5   Attitudes to finding work, by pathways

Per cent disagree

	Pathway 1 education	Pathway 2 educ. & other	Pathway 3 other all year
Unemployed young people haven't tried hard enough and don't know how to sell themselves	54	63	60 *
People like me find it difficult to get good jobs no matter how much education we have	27	28	30 *
Weighted sample, longitudinal sample	*1,148*	*187*	*251*

* p<.05

statement that people like them found it difficult to get jobs no matter how much education they had. It might be that this pattern of results is related, at a broader level, to a generally more positive outlook by those on the full-time education pathway. We have already found that they were more satisfied with what they were doing and gave positive reasons for choosing their initial destination at age 16.

Looking ahead

Respondents' perceptions of their prospects for the next few months were assessed in different ways according to their activity at the time of the third wave of data collection, and it is not possible to split their responses according to the pathway followed. However, we can get a general impression of how some respondents felt about the future depending on their activity at Wave 3 – if they were still in full-time education, or if they were working. Those in full-time training and those without a full-time activity were not asked.

Those who were still in full-time education by the end of the year, which was, of course, the majority of respondents, believed that they would either still be at college (42 per cent) or would be at university (31 per cent) six months after their present course finished. Given the relatively disadvantaged nature of this population, it is a very positive finding that so many thought that university was a possible option and reflects a general widening of the higher education net. It is worth noting that Asian respondents were particularly likely to be aiming to continue studying beyond the end of their current course, over four-fifths stating this as their intention, compared with 68 per cent of Black and 59 per cent of white students. Thus young people from ethnic minorities are not only more likely than whites to stay on at 16, they seem also more likely to continue participating in further and higher education. Again, young white people were more likely at this later stage to attempt to enter the labour market either as a trainee or an employee. Nineteen per cent of the white young people currently studying, intended to move directly into the labour market at the end of their course, compared with 11 per cent of Black and 10 per cent of Asian students.

Those who were working were also relatively positive about the immediate future. A large proportion (44 per cent) felt that their future job prospects were 'quite good', and a further 21 per cent felt that they were 'very good'. Most of the remainder were not sure (25 per cent) and only 10 per cent felt their prospects were bad.

Thus, for those who had successfully negotiated either the full-time education or the full-time employment routes, they not only felt positive about their choices but, in addition, they were hopeful about their future.

Conclusion

Simply staying on in education was not, on its own, a guarantee of good experiences over the year. However, for those who actively chose to stay on, and who managed to keep up with classes and complete a full year, this pathway was a successful one. They tended to feel most positively about their experiences, to be happy with what they were doing, and to feel that the immediate future was fairly secure. Similarly, for those in full-time work by the end of the year, the future was positively rated.

However, for the minority of people who dipped in and out of different activities throughout the year, the picture was not quite as positive. They had more negative views concerning activities such as youth training, and were prepared to feel that any job at all was better than doing nothing, implying fairly low levels of aspiration engendered, perhaps, by bad experiences. Many had made changes in their activities during the year for negative reasons such as dissatisfaction and money problems. They were less likely to report that teachers and parents had given them very helpful advice. The research project left them at the end of one year post-compulsory education; further research is crucial to establish what happens over a longer period of time to young people who follow these routes.

Problems and pressures

The first wave of *Changing Lives* contained data on the young people's perception of the extent to which they had suffered 'unfair treatment and discrimination'; the second wave included a question on a broader range of problems to do with money, family, and work; and the third wave covered questions on racism and the police. This chapter brings together some of these themes and also looks at the problems and pressures faced by certain small but important sub-groups of the sample, such as those who had experienced persistent unemployment over the year.

Problems and pressures

In the second wave, respondents were presented with a list of eight different types of problem that they may have faced since leaving Year 11. *Changing Lives 2* reported that more than 80 per cent of the sample indicated having faced one or more of those listed. Most frequently, this was debt or money problems, problems with their current activity or family problems. Reanalysing these data for the longitudinal sample produced similar results. Table 9.1 shows the problems encountered over the year. For each problem, two results are presented. The first is the number of respondents who identified the problem. The second is the proportion of the total problems identified (2,642, an average of approximately two per case) that each accounts for.

Respondents who wrote additional comments on their question-naires confirmed that these were indeed important issues. Thus, with respect to family difficulties, one wrote, 'Well at the moment, my mother and I are not speaking to one another ... I feel as if I have been rejected by the way I am treated. I am even thinking of leaving home because of this situation', while another commented, 'People look on

Table 9.1   Problems encountered over the year: longitudinal sample

Problem	Per cent of respondents	Proportion of all problems
Debt or money	43	22
With occupation	37	18
Family	32	16
Relationships	31	16
Finding occupation	28	14
Health	15	8
Housing/homelessness	5	3
Other	7	3

Weighted base, longitudinal sample, n=1,322

teenagers as a waste of space and treat us like we are kids with tantrums, when some of us have real problems and need help. So now I just depend on myself.' A third summarised 'the main and common problems', as being, '(1) we are not getting grants or not getting enough money, and (2) most of us want to get away from our relatives (parents) and live on our own and that is a problem'.

Results presented in the previous chapter suggested that those on the middle pathways, involving dipping in and out of education together with other activities, were the least happy of the groups. Was this also the group with the most problems? Table 9.2 shows how often each of the different problems was mentioned by those following the three main pathways, and summarises how many of each group mentioned at least one problem.

Those in the middle group reported the highest level of problems overall, particularly reflecting debt and money problems, family problems, and relationship problems. Those in the second and third groups reported equal rates of difficulty in finding work, two-fifths having found this to be a problem (42 per cent), while an equal proportion (43 per cent) of those involved in full-time study had had difficulties with the course. In comparison, between a quarter (25 per cent) and a fifth (19 per cent) of those not in full-time education reported difficulties with their current activity.

Table 9.2   Problems reported, by pathway taken

Per cent of respondents

Problem	Pathway 1	Pathway 2	Pathway 3
Debt or money	40	58	46
Housing	3	12	13
Family	32	37	31
Health	16	17	13
Finding work	22	42	42
With current activity	43	25	19
Relationships	32	36	26
Other	10	5	3

Weighted base, longitudinal sample, n=1,322

Racism and the police

Half of the *Changing Lives* respondents came from ethnic minorities. Not only do large proportions of young people get into trouble with the police at some point during their teens (up to 60 per cent in recent accounts, eg. Junger Tas, 1994), but people from ethnic minorities are more likely than white people to be stopped by the police (Smith, 1995), some estimates suggesting that this is twice as likely to happen to them (Smith and Gray, 1985). Some form of police contact was therefore likely to have been part of the general experiences of the young people during the year in which the study took place.

In the second questionnaire we offered respondents a choice of topics, the most popular of which we included in the third wave. Respondents chose racism and the police from a list that included drugs and alcohol, and HIV and AIDs issues. The responses to these questions reveal much about the experiences and attitudes of young people growing up in English cities, and this section summarises some of the main findings.

When asked if they had been stopped or questioned by the police in the last year, over a fifth (22 per cent) of the sample responded that they had. Figure 9.1 shows the variation in these rates for different ethnic groups.

Young men were three times as likely to have been stopped as young women (37 per cent compared with 12 per cent), and for both groups, those who were unemployed were twice as likely to have been stopped as those in full-time education. Nearly four in ten of the young men

Figure 9.1   Stopped or questioned by the police during the past year,
by ethnic origin and gender

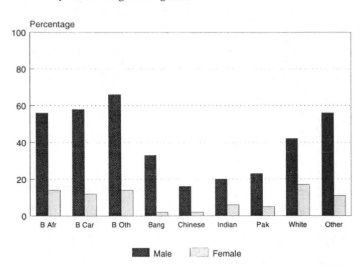

had been stopped, but for men from Black ethnic groups, the proportion was well over 50 per cent, and in the case of Black Others it approached two-thirds. By contrast, the proportion for young men of all Asian origins was just over a quarter in total. Of the young women, those of Black Caribbean or Black Other origin were most likely to have been stopped or questioned.

Usually, respondents had only been stopped once or twice in the year, and this was particularly the case for the young women. However, nearly a fifth (18 per cent) of the young men reported being stopped 11 or more times (this includes a minority who reported 'hundreds of times' or 'all the time'). The attitude of the police on these occasions is summarised in Figure 9.2.

The young women perceived the police to have been considerably more polite to them, although it should be remembered that young women were more likely to have only been stopped once or twice. In terms of ethnic differences, Indian and white young men appeared to receive more polite treatment than all other ethnic groups.

Respondents were then asked whether they felt the police harassed different ethnic groups. They rated whether they strongly agreed, agreed, were not sure, disagreed or strongly disagreed with three statements concerning harassment of Black people and Asian people.

Figure 9.2 How polite the police were, by gender

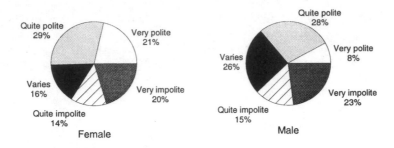

Female

Male

The percentages of each of the ethnic groups strongly agreeing with these statements are shown in Figure 9.3.

Only a minority of young white people strongly agreed that the police harassed young Black people more than their white counterparts, compared with one third of Black and half of Asian respondents. One fifth of Black respondents and two-thirds of Asian respondents believed that the police harassed Asian people more than white people. In both

Figure 9.3 'The police harass young Black people/young Asian people more than young white people' by ethnic group

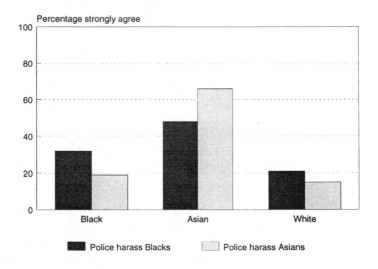

cases, each ethnic group believed that its group was the most harassed, but the Asians expressed more overall agreement that the police harassed ethnic minorities.

In addition to looking at these overall problems and pressures faced by sample members, we were also interested in the experiences of certain sub-groups who showed evidence of particular disadvantage throughout the year. The next sections look at who fell into these groups, and the types of experiences they faced.

Persistent unemployment

As we have already seen, unemployment was measured at each wave. A small group of respondents rated themselves as unemployed at each time point and, of these, a total of 92 rated themselves as unemployed on more than one occasion. Who were these young people and what sorts of experiences had they had of the year? Two-thirds of them (69 per cent) were female. They were fairly evenly spread across the six TEC areas, with between eight and 20 coming from each area. The numbers were too small to identify whether certain TECs were over-represented among the group. Confirming our earlier conclusion that entry into the labour market was more likely to be attempted by those from the white group than by ethnic minorities, 70 per cent of this persistently unemployed group were white (compared with 48 per cent of the whole sample).

As expected, as a whole the group had depressed GCSE results, with half (54 per cent) having failed to achieve any pass at all. However, interestingly, one quarter (25 per cent) had between one and four GCSEs graded A, B or C, so failure at GCSE was not necessarily a prerequisite for persistent unemployment. Rather more than average of this group, however, had been persistent truants at school, with just under half (48 per cent) missing substantial proportions of time in their last two years.

Respondents who were not in full-time activities at the time of the third wave were asked what sorts of things were preventing them from finding full-time work, training or study. The responses of this group are shown in Table 9.3.

Simply not being able to find a job was obviously the main reason for being without a full-time activity, but the rates of response to the remaining items suggests that there are, among this group, relatively large proportions of lone parents and those who are ill or injured.

Table 9.3   Reasons for lack of full-time activity among the persistently unemployed

Reason	Per cent of group citing reason
I can't find a full-time job	55
I have a child/children to look after	11
I am waiting for a course to start	11
I am ill or injured at the moment	7
I can't get a training place	5
My family won't let me	5
I have a disability	1
Other reasons	10

Weighted base 92

Respondents could choose multiple options

A quarter of the group had spent at least part of the year in some form of education, and 26 per cent of them turned out to have followed Pathway 2, which would have included other activities plus at least one month of education. The remainder (74 per cent) followed the 'Other all year' pathway. For 17 cases, a pathway could not be allocated due to missing information.

Family pressures: those not living with a parent

We also decided to look in more detail at who constituted the group of 101 young people not living with a parent. Nineteen of this group were also in the persistently unemployed group.

The proportion of young women in this group was again high, at 76 per cent compared with 57 per cent in the sample as a whole. The spread across the TECs was more irregular than it had been for the persistently unemployed, with a minimum of four coming from the Birmingham area, and a maximum of 26 from the Manchester area. An interesting contrast to the unemployed group was provided by looking at the ethnic origins of those not living with a parent – in this case just under half (49 per cent) were white, and over 30 per cent were Black.

The GCSE scores of this group were, on the whole, better than those of the unemployed and closer to those for the group as a whole. Thirty-one per cent had not achieved any GCSE results, a third had between one and four A-C grades. They were also less likely than the unemployed group to have been persistent truanters at school (40 per cent). Over a third (39 per cent) had followed the education all year option (compared with 72 per cent of the whole group), 22 per cent had followed either Pathways 2 or 3, and 40 per cent had been engaged in activities other than education all year.

Conclusion

In this inner-city sample of young people in their first year after compulsory education, money problems and debt headed the list of pressures encountered, and many had had some sort of contact with the police. Difficulties with money and debt were most apparent in the group who followed pathways dipping in and out of various activities, including education. Generally, the group who had stayed in full-time education were the least troubled, adding to the picture already painted in the previous chapters, which suggested that they were the happiest with their situation.

Two groups whose situation indicated multiple disadvantage were singled out for further study; the persistently unemployed and those who were not living with a parent. Despite a small overlap between the groups and the fact that they shared the characteristic of being predominately female, their profiles were quite different. The former was largely white and unqualified, and reported simply that they could not find work. A minority of them turned out to be lone parents. The second group was more ethnically representative and had slightly better examination results, but its members were nevertheless more likely to be following the more problematic pathways through the year.

10

Conclusion: changing lives for the better?

Focusing on young people from six inner-city areas, the *Changing Lives* study aimed to untangle some of the main pathways taken, and issues faced, by a group of potentially disadvantaged 16 year olds in the first year after the end of their compulsory education. Thirty-four schools took part, and over 3,000 young people answered questionnaires. A core of 1,980 provided longitudinal information over the course of the year.

Research summary

The results both confirmed other reports from nationally representative samples, and provided additional information about certain sub-groups.

- Over half of the respondents (53 per cent) belonged to an ethnic minority. The majority of the ethnic minority respondents were from Asian groups (38 per cent), and the remainder from Black groups (13 per cent).

- Over half the respondents were young women (57 per cent). The majority of the whole group were living at home with their parents (94 per cent), and the largest sections of the sample came either from families where the head was not working, or from the semi/unskilled sector.

- As expected, the *Changing Lives* sample achieved fewer GCSEs at the higher grades than national figures for the same year. Various factors seemed to be related to achievement. Confirming other recent reports, the young women scored better. The results for those from ethnic minorities varied with Chinese and Indian respondents achieving the highest scores, and Black Other and Black Caribbean respondents scoring the least well.

- Higher truancy rates were reported than for national samples, but most respondents held generally positive views of school. Both these factors varied by ethnicity and school attended, but in neither case did they vary by gender.

- Sessions with the local Careers Service were rated as the most useful source of careers advice, in preference to school based services. Parents and friends frequently provided informal advice.

- The majority of respondents opted to stay in some form of education at 16. Over three-fifths (71 per cent) were still in full-time education by the spring of the following year. This was despite the fact that the academic achievements of the *Changing Lives* sample were considerably depressed in comparison to their national peers.

- More than one in four of those in full-time education all year also had a part-time job at some point.

- Merging the three waves of the survey provided us with information on activities during each month of a 15 month period from April 1993 to June 1994. Three pathways taken by the sample, post-compulsory education, were identified. The first was the pathway of continuing full-time education, followed by three quarters of the longitudinal sample. The second involved some full-time study during the course of the year with other activities in addition. Eleven per cent followed this rather unsettled pathway, the vast majority of them starting off in education before moving off into other activities during the year. The final pathway, followed by 15 per cent, involved activities all year other than studying.

- Whether or not respondents followed different pathways depended in part on whether their GCSEs were sufficient, and how they got on at school in general. Two other main factors influenced which pathway was taken. The first was ethnicity, in that Asian students were more likely to stay on in full-time education than other ethnic groups. There were no differences between white and black groups in this respect. The second was the TEC area in which the respondent's school was based. In some TECs, more chose some pathways than in others.

- Following the final pathway of other activities all year was more likely for white respondents than other ethnic groups. White respondents were more likely to have had some full-time employment during the year in question.

- Experiencing at least one month of training was more likely for black respondents than for those from other ethnic groups. Other reports have suggested that training (rather than education or employment) can be the least positive option, particularly if the training is not employer based.

- Exploring respondents' experiences of the year suggested that those in education were the happiest with their choice, followed by those who had left education completely, particularly those in full-time work. Those who combined education with other activities were the least satisfied. This group also reported more problems and pressures throughout the year.

- A small group of 92 respondents were identified as persistently unemployed throughout the year. They were more likely to be young women, to be white and to be unqualified. They reported that they simply could not find work. Their qualifications were depressed although the group included some who had achieved good GCSE results. One in ten was a lone parent.

- A second sub-group, of those not living with a parent, were also analysed separately. This group was split between the ethnic minority groups and the white respondents. Examination results for the group were slightly better than for the persistently unemployed, but its members were still more likely to be following the more problematic pathways through the year.

Conclusions and policy implications

Things have been changing dramatically for young people over recent decades. As Banks et al (1992) concluded as a result of an earlier survey at the end of the 1980s, 'Some at least were poised to enter a decade of opportunity: others were facing exceptionally difficult problems in gaining employment. Most school leavers faced choosing between a variety of training schemes rather than the full-time jobs they had traditionally entered...Who you were and where you lived were crucial in determining where you went' (p28). At least in the short term, the majority of young people facing these difficult choices are opting to stay on in education.

There is no doubt that this is still on the increase, and in this sample of inner-city young people, staying on in education seemed to be the best option. Although earlier school performance was a strong predictor of whether or not they stayed on, in general their overall school performance was not striking and many who may previously have not been considered for further education were now continuing to study. It should not be assumed, however, that staying on was necessarily a positive choice, it was simply the best of the options open to them. It may only delay the point when they have to face the depressed employment market and in many cases it was leading to money and debt problems. Many were following vocational courses and it is crucial that the content of the further education received by this group is specifically tailored for the type of market they will have to enter at some point. The best education is going to be that which prepares them for their final career destination. Some expressed doubt in the relevance of their courses for 'life'. Already advantaged by better examination results, Asian students were the most likely to remain in education, even after controlling for differences in school achievement. This may have been due, in part, to differences in aspirations and family pressures; it may also have been partly because they did not feel confident about testing the job market.

Those who had followed the traditional pathways, leaving school at 16, were more likely to be white. This pathway was not necessarily a positive course, and those taking it were less satisfied than those on the education track. Those on this path were more likely to have had poor school records and to have been persistent truanters. However, some had found full-time work. The attendant financial rewards were likely to be the envy of many in the study, several of whom specifically listed debt as a problem and who wrote asking us to help them to find work.

It seems that the most nebulous of the pathways, retaining some investment in further education but also doing training, or other activities, during the year, was the least desirable. Those on this path were the least satisfied.

The picture is complicated. It is not easy to identify the 'winners' and the 'losers' in the pattern drawn by these analyses. We would need to continue to track the experiences of this group for many years to draw any conclusions about which pathways were the most protective given the initial starting point. Some groups seem more likely to try different things, some perhaps feel that more options are open to them even if these options are not very satisfactory.

Three main issues arise from these findings. The first is the question of how relevant are the alternatives to working for 16 year olds. It is likely that many of these young people would have liked to have been in the employment market but it was no longer an option for them. Whatever they do instead needs to be a relevant and useful alternative. Simply using education and training as 'holding' devices is likely just to postpone the point at which the problems begin, and increase the weight on both the local and broader community. In addition, if a significant minority of those staying on at school are those who would not, in the past, have considered further education to be an option (for example, because of lack of examinations), particular support is necessary to help them complete the year of studying. Careers guidance professionals must play a role here in ensuring that the most potentially vulnerable young people are directed only to suitable courses with realistic aims. Many respondents were obviously finding their courses much more difficult than anticipated, and those who had dropped out reported being least satisfied with what they were doing.

Second, the question of financial support throughout the teenage years is one that is becoming an increasing burden. In the inner city areas in which these young people live, the potential for income generation is small and decreasing. Some were obviously taking YT for the financial rewards, such as they are, rather than with any idea of using it as a stepping stone to something better. This may work in the short term but is likely, once again, simply to postpone the problem of developing a self-supporting lifestyle. A significant proportion of those in full-time education also had part-time jobs, perhaps increasing stress and chances of not being able to finish the course.

Third, ethnicity remains a significant predictor of pathways followed even after accounting for already existing variations between the ethnic groups by the end of their compulsory education. We do not have direct evidence of discriminatory practices at work in training nor employment, but it is most likely that they still exist. In addition, in increasingly competitive local conditions in the inner cities, the aspirations and expectations of certain ethnic minorities may be being eroded to the point where they do not feel it is worth even trying to exercise options other than education and training.

To conclude, it is crucial to continue to track the pathways and experiences of particular sub-groups of the population, as well as to look at national patterns. It is in these groups that changes to choices and options have most effect, and may highlight existing difficulties and disadvantages. Further research is needed following up samples such as that studied here, over a period of many years as they negotiate entry into the labour market.

Notes

1   This statistical test (analysis of variance) is used to test whether the mean level of one group is different from the mean level of another group or groups, to a greater extent than expected by chance. In effect, the distributions of the scores of the various groups are compared, because the spread of the scores will affect how much overlap there is between the groups. If there is a great deal of overlap (indicated by large standard deviations) the means will have to be further apart to be significantly different from each other. The 'p' value (probability) indicates how statistically significant these differences are. The less probable it is that the differences are due to chance fluctuations, the more confident one can be that there is a real difference between the groups. A 'p' value of .05 or less indicates that the likelihood of a result arising by chance is approximately 5 per cent or less. In other words, it is 95 per cent likely that the difference reflects a real difference. A probability of greater than .05 is usually treated as non-significant, as it implies that chance could have played role in the results. In general, for ease of presentation, only the probability levels of statistical tests are included in the text. Readers should contact the author for further details.

2   Where two LEAs are represented within a single TEC area, an average of the two authorities' scores has been recorded.

References

Banks M, Bates I, Breakwell G, Bynner J, Emler N, Jamieson L and Roberts K (1992) *Careers and Identities* Milton Keynes: Open University Press

Barber M (1993) *Raising Standards in Deprived Urban Areas,* National Commission on Education Briefing No. 16 London: National Commission on Education

Barber M (undated) *Young people and their attitudes to school* An interim report of a research project in the Centre for Successful Schools, Keele University

Beishon S, Virdee S and Hagell A (1995) *Nursing in a Multi-ethnic Society* London: PSI

Brown, C (1984) *Black and White Britain: The Third PSI Survey* London: Heinemann Educational Books

Bynner J and Roberts K (Ed) (1991) *Youth and Work: Transition to Employment in England and Germany* London: Anglo-German Foundation

Casey B and Smith D (1995) *Truancy and Youth Transitions* London: Department for Education and Employment Research Series Youth Cohort Report No.34

Chatrik B and Maclagan I (1995) *Taking Their Chances: Education, Training and Employment Opportunities for Young People* London: The Children's Society

Coleman J and Hendry L (1990) *The Nature of Adolescence* London: Routledge

Commission for Racial Equality (1993) *Choice, Diversity and Equality: A position paper on the Education Bill* London: CRE

Connolly M, Roberts K, Ben-Tovim G and Torkington P (1992) *Black Youth in Liverpool* The Netherlands: Giordano Bruno Gulemborg

Courtenay G and McAleese I (1993) *Cohort 5: aged 16-17 in 1991. Report on Sweep 1* London: Employment Department Research Series Youth Cohort Report No.22

Cross M, Wrench J & Barnett S (1990) *Ethnic minorities and the Careers Service: An investigation into processes of assessment and placement* London: Department of Employment Research Paper No.73

DES (1985) *The Swann Report*

DfE Statistical Bulletin Issue No 7/94 (June 1994)

Drew D and Gray J (1991) 'The black-white gap in examination results: a statistical critique of a decade's research'. *New Community,* 17, 159-172

Drew D, Gray J and Sime N (1992) *Against the Odds: The education and labour market experiences of young black people* London: Employment Department Research Series Youth Cohort Report No.68

Erikson E (1968) *Identity: Youth and Crisis* London: Faber & Faber

Evans K and Heinz RW (1994) (Eds) *Becoming Adults in England and Germany* London: Anglo-German Foundation

Hagell A and Newburn T (1994) *Persistent Young Offenders* London: Policy Studies Institute

HMI (1992) *The implementation of the pilot training credit scheme in England and Wales* London: Dept of Education

Jones T (1993) *Britain's Ethnic Minorities* London: Policy Studies Institute

Junger Tas J (1994) *Delinquent behaviour among young people in the Western world* Amsterdam: Kluger Publications

Kerckhoff AC (1990) *Getting Started: Transition to adulthood in Great Britain* Boulder CO: Westview Press

Lynn P, Purdon S, Hedges B and McAleese I (1994) *An assessment of alternative weighting strategies* London: Employment Department Research Series Youth Cohort Report No.30

Maughan B & Rutter M (1986) 'Black pupils' progress in secondary schools II: Examination achievements'. *British Journal of Developmental Psychology*, 4, 19-29

Meager N and Williams M (1994) *The case for national 'Equality in employment targets': A consultation paper prepared for TEC National Council* Brighton: Institute of Manpower Studies

Modood T, Beishon S and Virdee S (1995) *Changing Ethnic Minorities* London: Policy Studies Institute

Modood T and Shiner M (1994) *Ethnic Minorities and Higher Education* London: Policy Studies Institute

National Commission on Education (1993) *Learning to Succeed* London: Heinemann

O'Keefe DJ (1993) *Truancy in English Secondary Schools* London: HMSO

Payne J (1995a) *Routes beyond compulsory schooling* London: Employment Department Research Series Youth Cohort Report No.31

Payne J (1995b) *Qualifications between 16 and 18: A comparison of Achievements on Routes Beyond Compulsory Schooling* London: Employment Department Series Youth Cohort Report No.32

Penn and Scattergood (1992) 'Ethnicity and career aspirations in contemporary Britain', *New Community*, 19, 75-98

Rutter M, Maughan B, Mortimore P and Ouston J (1979) *Fifteen Thousand Hours: Secondary schools and their effects on children* Somerset: Open Books

Rutter M and Smith DJ (1995) *Psychosocial Disorders in Young People: Time trends and their causes* London: Wiley

Shaw C (1994a) *Changing Lives 1* London: Policy Studies Institute

Shaw C (1994b) *Changing Lives 2* London: Policy Studies Institute

Shaw C (1994c) *Changing Lives 3* London: Policy Studies Institute

Shiner M and Newburn T (1995) *Entry into the Legal Professions: The Law Student Cohort Study Year 3* London: The Law Society

Smith DJ (1995) 'Race, crime and criminal justice'. In M Maguire, R Morgan and R Reiner (Eds) *The Oxford Handook of Criminology* Oxford: Oxford University Press

Smith DJ and Gray J (1985) *Police and People in London* Aldershot: Gower

Smith DJ and Tomlinson S (1989) *The School Effect: A study of multi-racial comprehensives* London: Policy Studies Institute

Smith T and Noble M (1995) *Education Divides: Poverty and schooling in the 1990s* London: Child Poverty Action Group

Stares R, Imberg D and McRobie J (1992) *Ethnic Minorities* Manpower Services Commission Research Department, Series 6, London: MSC

The Times, 17 November 1993, School league tables

Tomlinson S (1990) 'Effective schooling for ethnic minorities' *New Community* 16, 337-347

Wilkinson RG (1994) *Unequal shares: The effects of widening income differentials on the welfare of the young* Ilford: Barnardos

Yates J (1994) *School Leavers Destinations 1993* London: ACC publications

Appendices

Appendix 1

Glossary of terms

This appendix was compiled in the process of background research for the project. Many of the terms appear in the report, others are included where we think them important to the issue even if they are not directly discussed in the book.

A-Level   Advanced level of the General Certificate of Education

BA   Bridging Allowance
            A discretionary allowance paid for a maximum of eight weeks (in a period of 52 weeks) to those who have left training or employment.

BTEC   Business and Technical Education Council qualification

Careers   Formerly called the Youth Employment Service. The
Service   Trade Union Reform and Employment Rights Act 1993 placed a duty on the Secretary of State to secure the provision of careers guidance and placing services for people attending schools and colleges, collectively termed the Careers Service. It is organised locally, as part of the responsibility of local government education departments. Usually it occupies separate premises and the staff are employed as professional careers counsellors.

CGLI   City and Guilds London Institute qualification

CPVE   Certificate of Pre-Vocational Education

CSE   Certificate of Secondary Education
            Merged with O-Levels into the GCSE in 1988.

DoE   Department of Employment, later became Employment Department (ED) and then Department for Education and Employment (DfEE)

DfE   Department for Education, later became DfEE

EMG   Ethnic Minority Grants
A grant, from the Home Office (announced in 1990), to be paid to voluntary organisations through TECs in order to assist minority ethnic groups by meeting particular employment, training and enterprise needs. In 1992-1993, TECs were allocated £4 million for EMG. 44 TECs got one.

GCSE   General Certificate of Secondary Education

GNVQs   General National Vocational Qualifications
For people still in education but with a vocational bias. Up to Level 3.
GNVQs saw the light of day in the May 1991 White Paper *Education and Training in the 21st Century.* Skills and knowledge from a particular vocational area are added to three core skills: communication, application of number and information technology. They are supposed to provide an alternative to A-levels, and a bridge between the academic and the vocational, offering preparation for higher education, work or 17/18+ vocational training. They were tried out in 1993 on over 8,000 candidates doing levels 2 or 3 in 100 further education colleges and schools. The most popular subject is Business, others include Manufacturing, Art and Design, Health and Social Care and Leisure and Tourism. The system is meant to be fully up and running and available to all schools and colleges in England and Wales, at least to level 3 (A-level equivalent) by autumn 1995. GNVQs replace, but only slightly augment, what BTEC National certificate and diploma have offered in further education. However, they can be taken in schools as well. GNVQ units (at level 1) are supposed to be available at key stage 4 of the national curriculum. The 12 vocational units that make up one level 3 GNVQ are supposed to be the equivalent of two A levels. As such, the intention is that such a GNVQ should allow interview at a university.

FHE Act   The Further and Higher Education Act 1992, giving FE
1992   colleges a wider role than previously.

HND   Higher National Diploma

LEA   Local Education Authority

LECs   Local Enterprise Companies

NVQs   National Vocational Qualifications
NVQs were an attempt to arrange 'the "jungle" of vocational awards within a common framework' (Evans & Heinz, 1994, p20). They are for people already in employment, and cover absolutely every type of work.
A NVQ is made up of a number of units that set certain standards that must be achieved. NVQs are awarded at several levels:
LEVEL 1 is competence in the performance of a range of work activities, most of which may be routine and predictable.
LEVEL 2 is competence in a significant range of work activities, some of which are complex or non-routine, and require some autonomy and responsibility.
LEVEL 3 is competence in a broad range of work activities performed in a wide variety of contexts, most of which are complex and non-routine.
LEVEL 4 is competence in a significant range of complex technical or professional work activities performed in a wide variety of contexts with a substantial degree of personal responsibility.

NCVQ   National Council for Vocational Qualifications

O-Level   Ordinary level of the General Certificate of Education taken at 16+
Merged with CSEs into the GCSE in 1988.

OND   Ordinary National Diploma

SHA   Severe Hardship Allowance
Normally paid to young people who are considered vulnerable and with no other form of support, for example, a homeless young person.

TCs   Training Credits
A Training Credit represents an entitlement for young people leaving full-time education to funding for structured training leading to recognised vocational

qualifications (NVQs or equivalent). Each TC enables a young person to have access to training for up to 104 weeks. It should be used within 12 months of the date of issue. The actual value depends on the costs involved in providing the relevant training programme and getting the qualification. They can only be used by young people with employers, colleges and training providers who are approved by the TEC. All 16-17 year olds are eligible. TCs are issued on behalf of the TEC by the Careers Service. All industrial sectors were covered by TCs from April 1992.

TECS   Training and Enterprise Councils
The establishment of TECs was announced in the Government's White Paper, *Employment for the 1990s.* TECs are employer-led organisations which are intended to plan and administer training and enterprise programmes (including youth training, adult learning, adult training, and enterprise allowance schemes), monitor skills shortages and design and deliver locally-based schemes which support and promote the development of small businesses.
Each TEC is established as a private limited company with a Board of Directors, of which two-thirds must be from the private sector. Board members may also be appointed from local education authorities, trade unions, and the voluntary sector.

TVEI   Technical and Vocational Education Initiative

YCS   Youth Cohort Study
The England and Wales YCS is a programme of research among 16-19 year olds designed to monitor their decisions and behaviour as they either stay on in full-time education or enter the labour market. The project is funded by the Department of Employment and the Department for Education, and is being conducted jointly by the Social and Community Planning Research (SCPR) and the QQSE Research Group in the Division of Education at Sheffield University.
The first cohort of people to be monitored were 16 in the school year 1983-1984 and were first surveyed in 1985.

The most recent cohort, Cohort 7, reached 16 in the school year 1992-1993, but results from this cohort are not available at the time of writing. Information about Cohort 6 (transitions 16-19) is published (Payne, 1994a and b). Samples are weighted to match population profiles for GCSE results, gender, region, school type and staying on in full-time education after 16.

YT   Youth Training

YT was introduced in May 1990. It is used by TECs and LECs to deliver training tailored to meet the needs of young people and businesses in their areas. YT replaced the YTS (Youth Training Scheme), which had given both employed and unemployed young people work-based and off-the-job training lasting up to two years which led to vocational qualifications. YT was intended to be more flexible, and to raise the numbers and levels of vocational qualifications achieved. YT is intended to improve broad-based skills, meet the skill needs of the local and national economy, and to provide training leading to NVQs at or above level 2. YT guarantees the offer of a suitable place to all 16 & 17 year olds leaving full-time education.

Appendix 2

Sample estimates unweighted and weighted

		Percentages
Variable	Unweighted	Weighted (Wave 1)
Gender		
Young men	43.0	43.3
Young women	57.0	56.7
Ethnicity		
Black African	4.4	4.4
Black Caribbean	6.2	6.6
Black Other	2.1	2.2
Bangladeshi	11.2	11.0
Chinese	2.4	2.2
Indian	8.5	8.2
Pakistani	14.2	13.8
White	47.7	48.4
Other	3.2	3.2
Year 11 GCSE results		
5+ A-C grades	28.1	22.7
1-4 A-C grades	38.7	38.1
5+ D-G grades	14.1	14.3
1-4 D-G grades	10.0	10.0
None	10.0	14.8

Appendix 3

Statistical notes:
Technical report on the logistic
regression analyses

Logistic regression is a form of multivariate analyses (ie, it involves more than two variables) where the dependent or response variable is dichotomous ('either/or'). Logistic regression can be used to predict the probability or odds that a person has a given characteristic (eg. have they found a training contract?) based on a combination of independent or predictor variables. The predictor variables can also be dichotomous (like male/female) or they can be continuous (like age). The probability of a respondent having followed any given pathway will always be between 0 and 1, where 0 means she will not, and 1 means she will. Odds measure the ratio of the probability that a characteristic will be present to the probability that it will be absent. Odds of 1, for example, indicate an even chance that a characteristic will be present.

In multivariate procedures, such as logistic regression, a whole range of independent variables can be held constant to allow us to estimate the influence of one particular variable, such as ethnicity. However, to do this, ethnicity itself must be broken down into a series of dichotomous variables where each different ethnicity is compared to a 'reference' group. In other words, white respondents' chances of having followed Pathway 1 were the base line against which the chances of Asian and Black respondents' were assessed. Thus, we can derive an estimate of the probability of following a particular pathway if the student is Asian, versus if the student is white, holding everything else that might vary constant, such as GCSE results, attitude to school, and truancy rates.

The version used was that to be found in a statistical software package for the social sciences called SPSS. Logistic regression produces odds-ratio estimates for each independent factor in the equation, rather than the least squares estimates produced by usual multiple regression techniques.

There are two reasons for some caution to be used in applying the results to the broader group of young people of this age. The first of these is that we have estimated the models on the basis of the weighted data and there are arguments for and against doing this. One argument against is that if some cases are weighted over 1, then the standard errors in the model may be falsely low, leading to an increased risk of finding statistically significant results. In order to provide some check that this was not happening in the present analyses, models were run on both weighted and unweighted data. For almost all variables in each of the three models the results were the same (although the coefficients obviously varied). The exceptions were that in the model for Path 2, the league position of the school was significant in the weighted data, whereas it was not in the unweighted data and whether a parent was in skilled employment was instead. In the Path 3 model, whether or not the school had a sixth form was significant in the unweighted data, but not in the weighted data. Thus, some minor variations were noted, but weighting did not alter the general pattern of results.

The second reason for exercising some caution is that the sample was selected to represent a rather specific population: those in inner city schools in relatively deprived urban areas. The sample selection was not random, as schools were selected to give a picture of inner city disadvantage. It is important to note that we cannot generalise from this group to, for example, all inner-city schools, nor to all relatively deprived areas. We are fairly confident that the sample (particularly after weighting for response bias) is reasonably representative of inner city, multi-ethnic areas, but that is all, and conclusions should not be drawn about any other population on the basis of these results. The fact that the sample is not entirely random and that there is some clustering within the sample (sets of schools from certain areas, for example) means that the sampling errors might be affected. It is crucial that these results are replicated with other samples from this population.

The results for each of the three final models are presented in Tables A.1, A.2 and A.3.

Table A.1 Logistic regression results: Predicting Pathway 1

Variable	B	SE	Sig	Exp(B)
Asian	.5058	.1408	.0003	1.6583
Skilled	-.2679	.1179	.0230	.7650
GCSEs	.6930	.0489	.0000	1.9997
Likesch	-.8645	.2099	.0000	.4212
League	.6121	.1637	.0002	1.8444
Truancy	-.4298	.0773	.0000	.6507
TEC (area 1 reference)			.0365	
Area 2	-.5850	.1839	.0015	.5571
Area 3	-.4253	.1949	.0291	.6535
Area 4	-.2173	.2095	.2996	.8047
Area 5	-.2060	.1750	.2393	.8138
Area 6	-.3764	.2080	.0703	.6863
Constant	-.2502	.3611	.4883	

Table A.2 Logistic regression results: Predicting Pathway 2

Variable	B	SE	Sig	Exp(B)
Asian	-.5858	.2116	.0056	.5567
GCSEs	-.3324	.0653	.0000	.7172
League	.4193	.2078	.0436	1.5209
Truancy	.5321	.1129	.0000	1.7024
Constant	-2.1677	.3531	.0000	

Table A.3   Logistic regression results: Predicting Pathway 3

Variable	B	SE	Sig	Exp(B)
Gender	-3.418	.1682	.0421	.7105
Asian	-1.2171	.2241	.0000	.2961
Black	- .6260	.2640	.0177	.5347
Skilled	.4427	.1623	.0064	1.5569
GCSEs	- .6543	.0617	.0000	.5198
Likesch	.8121	.2416	.0008	2.2526
League	- .6755	.2603	.0094	.5089
Truancy	.2975	.1052	.0047	1.3464
TEC (area 1 reference)			.0013	
Area 2	- .2088	.2936	.4770	.8116
Area 3	.9911	.2778	.0004	2.6941
Area 4	.0954	.2969	.7479	1.1001
Area 5	.1125	.2535	.6570	1.1191
Area 6	.3493	.2824	.2161	1.4181
Constant	-1.1127	.4784	.0200	

Appendix 4

Copies of the questionnaires

The *Changing Lives* survey is being carried out by researchers at PSI, Britain's leading independent social research institute.

Our aim is to let people know what things are really like for young people, in Britain's cities, in the 1990s. We expect the survey results to get national attention - in the newspapers, on radio, and on television.

Everything you tell us will be treated as strictly private and confidential. We will not even know your name, unless you choose to tell us.

Answering the questions:

Most of the questions can be answered by putting a tick in a box

Like this ☑

Some questions ask you to write things in

WRITE IN: *LIKE THIS (CLEARLY)*

Please ignore the little numbers beside the boxes. They just help us to record what you say.

Please do your best to fill in the questionnaire and send it back today.

YOU AND YOUR SCHOOL

1. *Are you male or female?*
   (TICK ONE BOX)   Male ☐   Female ☐ (8)

2. *What is your date of birth?*
   WRITE IN: _____/_____/197____
                          day   month   year
                          (9-10)   (11-12)   (13)

3. *How many different secondary schools did you go to between years 7 and 11?*
   (TICK ONE BOX)   1 school only   ☐ (14)
                          2 schools   ☐
                          3 or more schools ☐

4. *Here are some good and bad things which young people have said about school. What do you think?* **PLEASE TICK A BOX FOR EACH** *to say whether you agree or disagree.*

	Agree	Disagree
School has made me feel I have something to offer	☐	☐ (15)
School has been a waste of time	☐	☐ (16)
School has taught me things which would be useful in a job	☐	☐ (17)

The next question is about which subjects you studied in Years 10 and 11 and any qualifications you gained. We should like to know about all your results, however well or badly you did.

5a. *Please fill in your GCSE subjects and results:*

Subject (WRITE IN)	Your GCSE results (TICK A BOX FOR EACH SUBJECT)			
	A,B,C	D,E,F,G	U	Not entered
_____(18-19)	☐	☐	☐	☐ (20)
_____(21-22)	☐	☐	☐	☐ (23)
_____(24-25)	☐	☐	☐	☐ (26)
_____(27-28)	☐	☐	☐	☐ (29)
_____(30-31)	☐	☐	☐	☐ (32)
_____(33-34)	☐	☐	☐	☐ (35)
_____(36-37)	☐	☐	☐	☐ (38)
_____(39-40)	☐	☐	☐	☐ (41)
_____(42-43)	☐	☐	☐	☐ (44)
_____(45-46)	☐	☐	☐	☐ (47)
_____(48-49)	☐	☐	☐	☐ (50)
_____(51-52)	☐	☐	☐	☐ (53)

5b. *If you gained any **other** qualifications in years 10 and 11 (e.g. NPRA, BTEC, City and Guilds, RSA, NVQ, GNVQ) please write them in below:*

Subject	Qualification (e.g. BTEC)
_____(54-55)	_____(56-57)
_____(58-59)	_____(60-61)
_____(62-63)	_____(64-65)
_____(66-67)	_____(68-69)
_____(70-71)	_____(72-73)

6a. *Did you ever play truant (bunk off) from school in Year 10 or 11?* (TICK ONE BOX)

Yes: for the odd day or lesson   ☐ (74)

                for particular days or lessons   ☐

                for several days at a time   ☐

                for weeks at a time   ☐

No: never   ☐

6b. *Apart from playing truant (bunking off), did you ever spend more than a week off school in Year 10 or 11 because you were:* (TICK AS MANY BOXES AS YOU NEED)

ill or injured   ☐ (75)

excluded or suspended   ☐ (76)

visiting family abroad   ☐ (77)

for other reasons   ☐ (78)   (please tell us what they were) _____

_____

No, never   ☐ (79)

7. *Listed below are some of the ways that young people get advice about what to do at the end of Year 11.* **PLEASE TICK A BOX FOR EACH** *to tell us how helpful you found it, or if you didn't do it at all.*

	Very helpful	Quite helpful	Not helpful	Didn't do this
Careers lessons at school	☐	☐	☐	☐ (8)
An interview with the careers officer	☐	☐	☐	☐ (9)
Talked to my parent/s or guardian/s	☐	☐	☐	☐ (10)
Talked to other relatives	☐	☐	☐	☐ (11)
Talked to friends	☐	☐	☐	☐ (12)
Talked to teachers at school	☐	☐	☐	☐ (13)
Talked to other people (Please write in who)	☐	☐	☐	☐ (14)

_____

_____

WHAT YOU HAVE BEEN DOING SINCE APRIL

We would like to know what you have been doing over the last 5 months. **PLEASE TICK A BOX FOR EACH MONTH** *to let us know what you were doing for most of the month.*

8a. *In April I was doing:*
- ☐ (15) full-time study at school/college
- ☐ full-time paid work
- ☐ full-time training (e.g. YT)
- ☐ none of these (e.g. part-time work, unemployed, something else)

8b. *In May I was doing:*
- ☐ (16) full-time study at school/college
- ☐ full-time paid work
- ☐ full-time training (e.g. YT)
- ☐ none of these (e.g. part-time work, unemployed, something else)

8c. *In June I was doing:*
- ☐ (17) full-time study at school/college
- ☐ full-time paid work
- ☐ full-time training (e.g. YT)
- ☐ none of these (e.g. part-time work, unemployed, something else)

8d. *In July I was doing:*
- ☐ (18) full-time study at school/college
- ☐ full-time paid work
- ☐ full-time training (e.g. YT)
- ☐ none of these (e.g. part-time work, unemployed, something else)

8e. *In August I was doing:*
- ☐ (19) full-time study at school/college
- ☐ full-time paid work
- ☐ full-time training (e.g. YT)
- ☐ none of these (e.g. part-time work, unemployed, something else)

9. *What are you doing now?* **PLEASE TICK ONE BOX, THEN FOLLOW THE DIRECTIONS WHICH TELL YOU WHERE TO GO NEXT.** (20)

- full-time at school, 6th form college or FE college ☐ NOW GO TO Q.10 (PAGE 5)
- full-time training (e.g. YT) ☐ NOW GO TO Q.12 (PAGE 6)
- full-time paid work ☐ NOW GO TO Q.15 (PAGE 7)
- unemployed ☐ NOW GO TO Q.22 (PAGE 8)
- waiting to start a job I've been offered ☐ NOW GO TO Q.22 (PAGE 8)
- waiting for a training place ☐ NOW GO TO Q.22 (PAGE 8)
- doing other things (PLEASE WRITE IN) ☐ NOW GO TO Q.22 (PAGE 8)

Please answer the questions on this page if you are in full-time education at school or college

10. *Where are you studying now?* (TICK ONE BOX)

the same school I was in for Year 11 ☐ (21)
another school ☐
a 6th form college ☐
an FE college (for people of all ages) ☐
somewhere else ☐ (PLEASE WRITE IN WHERE)_____

_____

11. *What qualifications are you working towards now?* (TICK AS MANY BOXES AS YOU NEED AND FILL IN THE DETAILS FOR EACH ONE)

Subjects (WRITE IN)

GCSE ☐ (22) _____

_____

A-LEVEL ☐ (23) _____

_____

BTEC ☐ (24) _____

_____

City & Guilds ☐ (25) _____

_____

NVQ/GNVQ ☐ (26) _____

_____

RSA ☐ (27) _____

_____

Other ☐ (28) (PLEASE WRITE IN WHAT THEY ARE) _____

_____

None ☐ (29) (PLEASE WRITE IN WHAT YOU ARE STUDYING)_____

_____

NOW PLEASE GO TO Q. 22 (PAGE 8)

Please answer the questions on this page if you are doing full-time training (e.g. YT)

12. *Looking at your training programme from beginning to end, which best describes the type of training that you are getting?* (PLEASE TICK ONE BOX)

It is all based at a work placement ☐ (30)

It is mostly based at a work placement
(with some time at a college/training centre) ☐

It is mostly based at a college or training centre
(with some work experience) ☐

It is all based at a college or training centre ☐

None of these ☐ (PLEASE WRITE IN WHERE

YOUR TRAINING TAKES PLACE)_____

13. *What work are you being trained to do? (Please tell us in as much detail as you can)*

WRITE IN: _____

_____ (31-32)

14. *What qualifications are you working towards?* (TICK AS MANY BOXES AS YOU NEED AND FILL IN THE DETAILS FOR EACH ONE)

Subjects (WRITE IN)

BTEC ☐ (33) _____

_____

City & Guilds ☐ (34) _____

_____

NVQ/GNVQ ☐ (35) _____

_____

RSA ☐ (36) _____

_____

Other ☐ (37) (PLEASE WRITE IN WHAT THEY ARE) _____

_____

None ☐ (38)

NOW PLEASE GO TO Q. 22 (PAGE 8)

Please answer the questions on this page if you are in full-time paid work

15. *What is the name of your job?*

WRITE IN: _____ (39-40)

16. *What work do you mainly do? (Please tell us in as much detail as you can).*

WRITE IN: _____

_____ (41-42)

17. *Are you working for an employer or self-employed?* **(TICK ONE BOX)**
Working for an employer ☐
Self-employed ☐   Don't know ☐ (43)

18. *What is your employer's main business (that is, what kinds of things do they make or do?) If you are self-employed, please tell us what you make or do.* **PLEASE TELL US IN AS MUCH DETAIL AS YOU CAN.**

WRITE IN: _____ (44-45)

19. *Do you get any training as part of your job?* **(TICK ONE BOX)**
Yes ☐   No ☐   Not sure ☐ (46)

20. *Are you currently working for any qualifications, e.g., NVQ, BTEC, City and Guilds, RSA, trade apprenticeship?* **(TICK ONE BOX)**
Yes ☐ (47)   **(PLEASE WRITE IN WHAT THEY ARE)**_____

_____

No ☐

21. *How did you find this job?* **(TICK ONE BOX)**
Through the careers office ☐ (48)
Through the job-centre ☐
A newspaper advert ☐
An advert in a shop-window ☐
By asking employers if they had any jobs ☐
By asking my family or friends if they knew of any jobs ☐
Through work experience when I was at school ☐
In another way ☐ **(PLEASE WRITE IN)**_____

NOW PLEASE GO TO Q. 22 (NEXT PAGE)

Everyone please answer

22. *Are you doing any part-time work at the moment?* (TICK ONE BOX)

Yes ☐ (49)
No ☐

23. *Are you doing any part-time training or study at the moment?* (TICK ONE BOX)

Yes ☐ (50)
No ☐

24. *Are you looking for a full-time or part-time job at the moment?* (TICK AS MANY BOXES AS YOU NEED)

Yes, full-time job ☐ (51)
Yes, part-time job ☐ (52)
No ☐ (53)

25. *Here is a list of things that people have said about jobs and training.* PLEASE TICK A BOX FOR EACH *to say how strongly you agree or disagree.*

	Strongly agree	Agree	Unsure	Disagree	Strongly disagree
A person must have a job to feel a full member of society.	☐	☐	☐	☐	☐ (54)
It is much better to get some kind of training than to go straight into a paid job.	☐	☐	☐	☐	☐ (55)
Having almost any job is better than being unemployed.	☐	☐	☐	☐	☐ (56)
Youth training schemes are just slave labour.	☐	☐	☐	☐	☐ (57)
Once you've got a job, it's important to hang on to it even if you don't really like it.	☐	☐	☐	☐	☐ (58)
If I didn't like a job I'd pack it in, even if there was no other job to go to.	☐	☐	☐	☐	☐ (59)
A person can get satisfaction out of life without having a job.	☐	☐	☐	☐	☐ (60)

26a. *How happy are you with what you are doing at the moment?* (TICK ONE BOX)

Very happy ☐ Quite unhappy ☐ (61)
Quite happy ☐ Very unhappy ☐
Neither happy nor unhappy ☐

26b. *What would you like to be doing 1 year from now?*

WRITE IN: _____ (62-63)

26c. *What would you like to be doing in five years time?*

WRITE IN: _____ (64-65)

MORE ABOUT YOU

Not all young people get the same chance to make use of their abilities. Race, class, sex, religion, disability, and the place where you live are just some of the things that might affect your opportunities. We need to ask the questions in this section to find out how these things affect young people's chances.

27a. *Which country were you born in?*

WRITE IN: _____ (66-67)

27b. *For how many years have you lived in Britain?* (TICK ONE BOX)

All my life	☐	5 to 9 years	☐ (68)
10 years or more	☐	Less than 5 years	☐

28. *How would you describe your ethnic origin?* (TICK ONE BOX)

Black African ☐ (69-70)
Black Caribbean ☐
Black Other ☐ (PLEASE WRITE IN DETAILS)_____

Bangladeshi ☐
Chinese ☐
Indian ☐
Pakistani ☐

White ☐

Other ☐ (PLEASE WRITE IN DETAILS)_____

29a. *Do you speak any other languages apart from English?* (TICK ONE BOX AND THEN WRITE IN)

Yes ☐   No ☐ (71)

29b. Which other language(s) do you speak?_____

_____

_____(8-13)

29c. Which language(s) do you speak at home?_____

_____

_____(14-19)

29d. Which language(s) do you speak with your friends?_____

_____

_____(20-25)

P R I V A T E

30. *What is your religion, if any?* (TICK ONE BOX)

Buddhist	☐	Hindu	☐ (26-27)
Christian:		Jewish	☐
Church of England	☐	Muslim	☐
Roman Catholic	☐	Rastafarian	☐
Other Christian	☐	Sikh	☐
Confucian	☐	No religion	☐

Other   ☐   (PLEASE TELL US WHAT) _____

31. *Do you have any physical difficulties that affect your life, for example, asthma, epilepsy, those kinds of things?* (TICK ONE BOX)

Yes ☐ (28)
No ☐

32. *Do you have any children of your own (whether or not they live with you at the moment)?* (TICK ONE BOX)

Yes ☐ (29)
No ☐

33. *Have you ever been treated unfairly for any of the reasons listed below?* (TICK AS MANY BOXES AS YOU NEED TO)

	Yes	No
because of your race or colour	☐	☐ (30)
because of the estate or area where you live	☐	☐ (31)
because of your sex	☐	☐ (32)
because of your religion	☐	☐ (33)
for other reasons	☐	☐ (34)

(PLEASE WRITE IN WHAT THEY WERE) _____

_____

_____

_____

_____

34. *Is there anything else that you would like to say?* (PLEASE WRITE IN)

_____

_____

_____

_____

_____

We would like to send you another questionnaire in about 4 months' time. To help us get in touch with you easily, please write your name, address and phone number below. If you prefer not to give your name and address to us, we will ask your school to send you a questionnaire.

Name _____

Address _____

_____

Postcode _____

Phone number (daytime) _____

(evenings) _____

If you think you might have moved by February 1994, please write down the name, address and phone number of someone who could help us get in touch with you (for example, a relative or good friend who is likely to know where you are).

Name _____

Address _____

_____

Postcode _____

Phone number (daytime) _____

(evenings) _____

Please tick the box below if you would like a copy of the survey results.

I would like a copy of the survey results ☐ (36)

Please put this booklet into the reply-paid envelope provided and post it off to us straight away. **It does not need a stamp.**

Thanks again for your help.

If you would like further information about the Changing Lives survey please contact: Catherine Shaw, Policy Studies Institute, 100 Park Village East, London NW1 3SR.

*The Changing Lives surveys are being carried out by researchers at PSI,
Britain's leading independent social research institute.*

*Our aim is to let people know what things are really like for young people, in
Britain's cities in the 1990s. We expect the survey results to get national
attention in the newspapers, on radio, and on television.*

This is the second booklet in a series of three.

*Everything you tell us will be treated as strictly private and confidential.
Only the researchers will ever know what you have said.*

How to answer the questions:

Most of the questions just need a tick in a box

Like this

A few questions ask you to write things in

Write in: C L E A R L Y

Please ignore the little numbers beside the boxes.

Please do your best to fill in the questionnaire and send it back today.

THANK YOU

What do you think?

Here are some things people have said about education, work and unemployment. Do you agree or disagree?
(Please tick one box for each statement)

	agree	neither	disagree	
1 a It is mainly a matter of luck whether a school-leaver gets a job or not	☐	☐	☐	(8)
1 b Unemployed young people haven't tried hard enough and don't know how to sell themselves.	☐	☐	☐	(9)
1 c Going to the right school and having the right contacts is a big part of getting a job.	☐	☐	☐	(10)
1 d It really doesn't matter how well you do at school.	☐	☐	☐	(11)
1 e Employers pay a lot of attention to school reports and examination results.	☐	☐	☐	(12)
1 f People like me find it difficult to get good jobs no matter how much education we have.	☐	☐	☐	(13)
1 g Some people require education for their jobs but for most of us it is a waste of time.	☐	☐	☐	(14)
1 h Failure in examinations ruins a person's chances in life.	☐	☐	☐	(15)

1

What have you been doing since October?

We would like to know what you have been doing over the last four months. Please tick one box for each month to let us know what you were doing for <u>most</u> of that month.

2 a   In October I was doing
      (tick one box)
      ☐ full-time study
      ☐ full-time paid work
      ☐ full-time training
      ☐ none of these (eg part-time work, unemployed, something else) (16)

2 b   In November I was doing
      (tick one box)
      ☐ full-time study
      ☐ full-time paid work
      ☐ full-time training
      ☐ none of these (eg part-time work, unemployed, something else) (17)

2 c   In December I was doing
      (tick one box)
      ☐ full-time study
      ☐ full-time paid work
      ☐ full-time training
      ☐ none of these (eg part-time work, unemployed, something else) (18)

2 d   In January I was doing
      (tick one box)
      ☐ full-time study
      ☐ full-time paid work
      ☐ full-time training
      ☐ none of these (eg part-time work, unemployed, something else) (19)

If there has been any change in what you have been doing since October please answer question 3, otherwise go straight to question 4.

3   What were the main reasons for the change(s)?
    (tick as many boxes as you need)
    (20)☐ I needed some money, or more money
    (21)☐ my personal circumstances changed (eg illness, pregnancy, moving house, getting married)
    (22)☐ I wasn't happy with what I was doing
    (23)☐ I had the chance to do something better
    (24)☐ I had no choice, other people made the decision
    (25)☐ other **(write in)**

....

Everybody please answer the next question:

4   What are you doing now? **(please tick one box and follow the instructions which tell you what page to go to next)**
    (26)☐ full-time study . . . . , ... **go to page 3**
    ☐ full-time work or training (over 30 hours per week). . . . .**go to page 5**
    ☐ other (eg unemployed, part-time work, looking after family etc) . . . . **go to page 7**

If you are studying full-time at school or college, please answer these questions.

5   Are you still following the same course(s) that you started in September?
    (please tick one box)
    ☐   yes
    ☐   no, I have changed course(s)   (27)

6   Please tell us what kind of qualifications you are working towards <u>now</u>
    (tick as many boxes as you need)
    ☐   GCSE re-sit(s)   (28)
    ☐   GCSE new subject(s)   (29)
    ☐   A level(s)   (30)
    ☐   A/S level(s)   (31)

    ☐   GNVQ *(now please tick one box to tell us which level)*   (32)
            ☐   foundation
            ☐   intermediate
            ☐   advanced
            ☐   not sure
    ☐   BTEC *(now please tick one box to tell us which level)*   (34)
            ☐   first
            ☐   National
            ☐   higher
            ☐   not sure
    ☐   NVQ *(now please tick one box to tell us which level)*   (36)
            ☐   level 1
            ☐   level 2
            ☐   level 3
            ☐   not sure
    ☐   other qualification(s) *(please write in)*   (38-39)

    ....
    ....
    ....

    ☐   none   (40)

7   Do you find the work on your course easier than you expected, about the same as
    you expected, or more difficult than you expected?
    (please tick one box)
    ☐   easier
    ☐   about the same
    ☐   more difficult   (41)

3

8   How are you managing to keep up with the workload? *(please tick one box)*

☐ I'm just about up-to-date with everything
☐ I'm a bit behind
☐ I'm very behind   (42)

9   Do you attend all your classes? *(please tick one box)*

☐ Yes, always
☐ I've missed a few classes
☐ I sometimes miss a day
☐ I quite often miss a day or two
☐ I hardly ever attend   (43)

10 Do you receive a maintenance grant from your Local Education Authority?
    (please tick one box)

☐ yes
☐ no
☐ not sure   (44)

11 For some courses, students need to buy special equipment (eg art materials, chef's
    knives, hairdressing scissors) or text-books. How does this affect you?
    (please tick one box)

☐ I don't need to buy anything like that
☐ I work part-time to pay for things like that
☐ My grant pays for things like that
☐ My parent(s) pay for things like that
☐ I need things like that but I just can't afford to buy them   (45)

12 Is work experience part of your course? *(please tick one box)*

☐ yes
☐ no
☐ not sure   (46)

13 When does your course finish? *(please tick one box)*

☐ summer 1994
☐ summer 1995
☐ part summer 1994, part summer 1995
☐ other   (47)

now please go to page 8

4

If you are in <u>full-time work or training</u>, please answer these questions

14 What kind of work are you doing or being trained to do? *(please write in)*

....
....
....(48-4

15 In this full-time job/training, how many hours do you work/train altogether in a normal week? *(write in)*

.... hours a week (50-5

16 Where do you spend your time in this job/training? *(please tick one box)*

☐ all at a workplace
☐ mostly at a workplace
(with some time at college or training centre)
☐ mostly at a college or training centre
(with some time at a workplace)
☐ all at a college or training centre   (53)

17 Overall, how satisfied are you with the training you receive? *(please tick one box)*

☐ very satisfied
☐ fairly satisfied
☐ not very satisfied
☐ not at all satisfied
☐ I don't get any training   (54)

If you are on YT, please answer question 18, otherwise go to question 19

18 How do you rate your chances of getting a job at the end of your training? *(please tick one box)*

☐ very good
☐ fairly good
☐ not sure
☐ not very good
☐ not at all good   (55)

now go to question 19

5

19 Have you taken time off from this job or training for any of the reasons given below? Don't include paid holiday or annual leave.
   (please tick as many boxes as you need)

☐ illness or injury (56)
☐ religious holidays (57)
☐ personal problems (58)
☐ because you didn't feel like going in (59)
☐ other reasons (write in) (60)

....

....

☐ I haven't taken any time off (apart from paid holiday or annual leave) (61)

20 What is your time-keeping like in this job or training?
   (please tick one box)

☐ I'm never late
☐ I'm hardly ever late
☐ I'm late at least once a week
☐ I'm late several times a week (62)

*The next 2 questions are about your pay. **Remember that this is a totally private and confidential survey.** We are only asking these questions in order to find out whether young people are getting fair pay for the jobs or training that they do. We will not pass this, or any other information in this questionnaire, to anybody else.*

21 We would like to know about your take-home pay from your full-time job or training. That is the amount of money you get for yourself after tax and National Insurance etc are deducted. Please tell us how much you take home in a normal week (tick one box)

☐ a training allowance of £29.50 (plus travel expenses) (63)
☐ a training allowance of £35.00 (plus travel expenses) (64)
☐ another amount (write in) (65)
£. . . . . .per week (66-70)

22 Do you get paid less if you are late or miss a day? (please tick one box)

☐ yes
☐ no
☐ not sure (71)

23 Do you pay for your board and lodging? (please tick one box)

☐ yes, £10 or less a week
☐ yes, between £11 and £20 a week
☐ yes, more than £21 a week
☐ no, I don't pay anything (72)

now please go to page 8

If you are <u>not doing full-time work, training or study at the moment</u> please answer the questions on this page.

There are lots of reasons why young people might not be doing full-time work, training or study. Sometimes they can't find what they want, sometimes their families won't let them do what they want, sometimes they are quite happy as they are. We'd like to know a bit more about what you are doing, and the reasons why.

24 Are you doing any of these things at the moment? *(tick as many boxes as you need)*

☐ part-time work (8)
☐ part-time study (9)
☐ part-time training (10)
☐ looking after home and family (11)

25 Would you **prefer** to be working, studying or training **full-time** if you had the chance? *(tick as many boxes as you need)*

yes: ☐ full-time work (12)
☐ full-time study (13)
☐ full-time training (14)
no: ☐ (15)

If you answered 'yes' to question 25, please answer question 26.
If you answered 'no' to question 25, please go straight to question 27.

26 What sorts of things are stopping you from doing full-time study, training or work at the moment? *(tick as many boxes as you need)*

☐ I can't find a full-time job (16)
☐ I can't find a full-time training place (17)
☐ I can't find a full-time course to do (18)
☐ my family won't let me (19)
☐ I am ill or injured at the moment (20)
☐ I have a disability (21)
☐ I have a child or children to look after (22)
☐ other reasons *(write in)*

.... (23-24)

....

27 Would you describe yourself as 'unemployed' at the moment?
(please tick one box)

☐ yes
☐ no
☐ not sure (25)

7

Everybody, please answer these questions

28 How happy are you with what you are doing at the moment?
(please tick one box)

☐ very happy
☐ quite happy
☐ neither happy nor unhappy
☐ quite unhappy
☐ very unhappy   (26)

Everybody has problems at one time or another in their lives. We are interested in finding out what kinds of problems young people have to face these days, and how they cope.

29 <u>Since finishing Year 11</u>, what kinds of problems have you had to face?
(please tick as many boxes as you need)

☐ debt or money problems   (27)
☐ housing problems or homelessness   (28)
☐ family problems   (29)
☐ health problems   (30)
☐ problems finding work, training or courses to do   (31)
☐ problems with your work, study or training   (32)
☐ relationship problems (boyfriend, girlfriend)   (33)
☐ other sorts of problems *(write in)*

.... (34)

....

30 <u>If you had problems</u>, what people or organisations were helpful to you?
(please tick as many boxes as you need)

☐ parents   (35)
☐ other relatives   (36)
☐ friends   (37)
☐ teachers, tutors, trainers or bosses   (38)
☐ Careers officers   (39)
☐ other professional people (eg doctor, social worker)   (40)
☐ people at your place of worship   (41)
☐ telephone helplines (eg Childline, Samaritans)   (42)
☐ other people/organisations *(please write in)*

.... (43)

....

☐ I tried to get help, but nobody could help me   (44)
☐ I didn't ask other people to help me   (45)

8

Everybody please answer these questions

Home and family

3 1 How much time do you normally spend each week doing housework (cooking, cleaning, shopping for food)? _(please tick one box)_

☐ I don't do this at all
☐ up to 5 hours a week
☐ 5–15 hours a week
☐ more than 15 hours a week   (46)

3 2 How much time do you spend each week looking after members of your family (eg younger brothers or sisters, old, disabled or sick relatives)? _(please tick one box)_

☐ I don't do this at all
☐ up to 5 hours a week
☐ 5–15 hours a week
☐ more than 15 hours a week   (47)

3 3 Here is a list of things young people have said about their families. Tick one box for each statement to show how strongly you agree or disagree

	strongly agree	agree	not sure	disagree	strongly disagree	
My family would support me in anything I decided to do	☐	☐	☐	☐	☐	(48)
My family are never happy with anything I do	☐	☐	☐	☐	☐	(49)
My family expect a lot of me	☐	☐	☐	☐	☐	(50)
My family don't really care what I do	☐	☐	☐	☐	☐	(51)

9

We will be sending out another questionnaire to you in June (it will probably be the last one). We would like to give you the chance to choose one of the topics.
Listed below are four important subjects which can have an impact on the lives of young people. Please select one, and next time we will include questions on the most popular choice.

3 4 I would like the next questionnaire to include questions on: *(please tick one box)*

☐ Crime and the police
☐ Drugs and alcohol
☐ HIV and AIDS
☐ Racism   (52)

Finally, we are asking the next two questions because we want to find out if young people today really are getting equal opportunities.

3 5 Are you male or female? *(tick one box)*

☐ male
☐ female
                                            (53)

3 6 How would you describe your ethnic origin? *(please tick one box)*

☐ Black African
☐ Black Caribbean
☐ Black Other *(write in)*   (55-56)
....

☐ Bangladeshi
☐ Chinese
☐ Indian
☐ Pakistani
☐ White
☐ Other *(write in)*
.... (57-58)

3 7 Is there anything else you would like to say? *(please write in)*

....
....
....

please turn over

10

We will be asking your school to send you the last questionnaire in this series in a few months time. If you think you might be moving in the next few months (between now and July 1994), please can you write down the name address and phone number of someone who could help us get in touch with you (for example a relative or good friend who is likely to know where you are).

Name   ....

Address   ....

                .... Post code ....

Phone number (daytime) ....

Phone number (evenings) ....

Now please put this booklet into the reply paid envelope provided and post it off to us straight away. It does not need a stamp.

THANKS AGAIN FOR YOUR HELP.

If you would like further information about the Changing Lives survey, please contact: Catherine Shaw, Policy Studies Institute, 100 Park Village East, London NW1 3SR.

The Changing Lives surveys are being carried out by researchers at PSI, Britain's leading independent social research institute.

Our aim is to let people know what things are really like for young people, in Britain's cities in the 1990s. We expect the survey results to get national attention in the newspapers, on radio, and on television.

This is the last in a series of three booklets.

Everything you tell us will be treated as strictly private and confidential. Only the researchers will ever know what you have said.

How to answer the questions:

Most of the questions just need a tick in a box

Like this   ☑

A few questions ask you to write things in

Write in: CLEARLY

Please ignore the little numbers beside the boxes.

Please do your best to fill in the questionnaire and send it back today.

THANK YOU

What have you been doing since February?

We would like to know what you have been doing since we sent the last questionnaire. *Please tick one box to show what you were doing for <u>most of each month:</u>*

1 a   In March I was doing (8)
      (tick one box)
      ☐ full-time study
      ☐ full-time paid work
      ☐ full-time training
      ☐ none of these (eg unemployed, doing something else)

1 b   In April I was doing (9)
      (tick one box)
      ☐ full-time study
      ☐ full-time paid work
      ☐ full-time training
      ☐ none of these (eg unemployed, doing something else)

1 c   In May I was doing (10)
      (tick one box)
      ☐ full-time study
      ☐ full-time paid work
      ☐ full-time training
      ☐ none of these (eg unemployed, doing something else)

2 a   Have you changed what you were doing between the month of February and now? *(please tick one box)*
(11)
      yes ☐ *(please answer question 2b)*
      no ☐   *(go straight to question 3)*

      2 b   What were the main reasons for the change?
            (tick as many boxes as you need)
(12)   ☐ I needed some money, or more money
(13)   ☐ my personal circumstances changed (eg illness, pregnancy, moving house, getting married etc)
(14)   ☐ I wasn't happy with what I was doing
(15)   ☐ I had the chance to do something better
(16)   ☐ I had no choice, other people made the decision
(17)   ☐ other *(write in)*
            ....
            (now please go to question 3)

3   And what are you doing now?
      (please tick the box which best describes what you are doing at the moment and follow the instructions which tell you which page to turn to next)
      full-time study at school/college (2year course) . . . . ☐ go to page 2
      just finishing a 1 year course at school/college . . . . ☐.go to page 2
      full-time paid work (over 30 hours per week). . . . . ☐ go to page 3
      full-time training eg YT . . . . ☐.go to page 4
(18) other (eg unemployed, looking after family etc) . . . . ☐go to page 5

page 1

If you are studying full-time, or have just finished a course, please answer these questions:

4   If you have had homework, revision or projects to do in your own time, where do you <u>usually</u> study? *(please tick as many boxes as you need)*

- (19) ☐ at home in my bedroom
- (20) ☐ at home in another room
- (21) ☐ at school or college
- (22) ☐ in the public library
- (23) ☐ at a friend's house
- (24) ☐ somewhere else *(write in)* ....
- (25) ☐ I never have this kind of work to do

5   Why did you decide to continue your education after year 11? *(please tick as many boxes as you need)*

- (26) ☐ that's what most of my friends were doing
- (27) ☐ I was really interested in the subject(s) I've been studying
- (28) ☐ my family wanted me to
- (29) ☐ I couldn't find a job
- (30) ☐ I need more qualifications for the job I want
- (31) ☐ I want to go to university eventually
- (32) ☐ it's better than being unemployed
- (33) ☐ I wanted to improve my qualifications
- (34) ☐ I didn't know what else to do
- (35) ☐ other reason *(please write in)*

....

6   What do you hope to be doing six months after your present course finishes? *(please tick one box and fill in details)*

- (36) ☐ working full-time
  (please write in what job)... (37-38)
- ☐ training for a job
  (please write in what job)... (39-40)
- ☐ further study at school/college
  (please write in what qualifications) ....(41-42)
- ☐ studying for a university degree
  (please write in what subject)..(43-44)
- ☐ other
  (please write in)..(45-46)
- ☐ not sure

now please go to page 6

page 2

If you are in full-time work, please answer these questions:

7a   What is your job?

(please write in).. (47-48)

7b   What is your employer's main business? What does the firm or organisation make or do?
(please write in)..

.... (49-50)

8   Are you a member of a Trade Union? *(please tick one box)*

(51) ☐ yes
     ☐ no
     ☐ not sure

9   How good do you think your prospects are in this job in terms of promotion, pay rises and more responsibility in the future? *(please tick one box)*

(52) ☐ very good
     ☐ quite good
     ☐ not sure
     ☐ quite bad
     ☐ very bad

10a What, if anything, do you <u>like</u> most about your job?

(write in).. (53-54)

10b What, if anything, do you <u>dislike</u> most about your job?

(write in)..(55-56)

11   Do you get any training as part of your job? *(please tick one box)*

yes: YT . . . . ☐ please go to page 4
       apprenticeship . . . . ☐ please go to page 6
       other training . . . . ☐ please go to page 6

no: . . . . ☐ please go to page 6 (57)

page 3

If you are in full-time training (eg YT), please answer these questions:

12 What kind of work are you being trained to do?

(please write in) .... (58-59)

13 Is this the kind of work you wanted to be trained for?
(please tick one box)

(60) ☐ yes
☐ I didn't really know what I wanted
☐ no *(please write in what you wanted)*

....

14 Did you buy your training using a 'Training Credit', Youth Credit or Futures card?
(please tick one box)

(61) ☐ yes
☐ no
☐ not sure

15a What, if anything, do you <u>like</u> most about your training?

(write in).. (62-63)

15b What, if anything, do you <u>dislike</u> most about your training?

(write in) .... (64-65)

16 Why did you decide to take a training course?
(please tick as many boxes as you need)

(66) ☐ that's what most of my friends were doing
(67) ☐ I was really interested in the work I've been training for
(68) ☐ my family wanted me to
(69) ☐ I couldn't find a job
(70) ☐ I'd had enough of school and studying
(71) ☐ I needed some money
(72) ☐ it's better than being unemployed
(73) ☐ I wanted to improve my qualifications
(74) ☐ It will help me get a better job in the end
(75) ☐ I didn't know what else to do
(76) ☐ other reason
(please write in) ....

now please go to page 6

If you are not doing full-time work, training or study at the moment, please answer these questions:

There are lots of reasons why young people might not be doing full-time work, training or study. Sometimes they can't find what they want, or other people may prevent them from doing what they want. And some people are quite happy as they are . . . what about you?

17 If you would <u>prefer</u> to be doing full-time work, training or study at the moment, what sorts of things are stopping you? *(please tick as many boxes as you need)*

(8) ☐ I can't find a full-time job
(9) ☐ I can't get a training place
(10) ☐ I am waiting for a course to start
(11) ☐ my family won't let me
(12) ☐ I am ill or injured at the moment
(13) ☐ I have a disability
(14) ☐ I have a child or children to look after
(15) ☐ other reasons
(write in)...

18 Are you doing any of these things at the moment?
(please tick as many boxes as you need)

(16) ☐ part-time work, study or training
(17) ☐ voluntary (unpaid) work or work experience
(18) ☐ helping out with the family business
(19) ☐ looking after home and family

19 What do you hope to be doing six months from now?
(please tick as many boxes as you need)

(20) ☐ full-time study
(21) ☐ part-time study
(22) ☐ full-time training
(23) ☐ part-time training
(24) ☐ full-time work
(25) ☐ part-time work
(26) ☐ looking after home/family
(27-28) ☐ other
(please write in)...

20 Would you describe yourself as 'unemployed' at the moment?
(please tick one box)

☐ yes
☐ no
(29) ☐ not sure

Everybody, please answer these questions:

21   How happy are you with what you are doing at the moment?
(please tick one box)

(20) ☐ very happy
☐ quite happy
☐ neither happy nor unhappy
☐ quite unhappy
☐ very unhappy

22a Do you have a <u>part-time</u> paid job or jobs at the moment?
(please tick one box)

(31) ☐ yes *(please answer questions 22b and 22c)*
☐ no *(please go straight to question 23)*

22b   What is your part-time job or jobs?

(write in)...(32-33)

22c   How many hours of <u>part-time</u> work do you do in a
<u>normal</u> week? *(please write in)*

.... hours

(34-35)

23   Are you looking for work at the moment?
(please tick as many boxes as you need)

(36) ☐ yes, full-time work
(37) ☐ yes, part-time work
(38) ☐ yes, a job for the summer holidays
(39) ☐ no

24   Who are you living with at the moment?
*When we say 'parent' 'brother' or 'sister' we mean whoever <u>you</u> think of as
being your parent, brother or sister*
(tick as many boxes as you need)

(40) ☐ parent(s)
(41) ☐ older brother/sister(s)
(42) ☐ younger brother/sister(s)
(43) ☐ other relatives
(44) ☐ my husband/wife/boyfriend/girlfriend
(45) ☐ relatives of my husband/wife/boyfriend/girlfriend
(46) ☐ my own child or children
(47) ☐ friend(s)
(48) ☐ another person or people
(49) ☐ no-one else, I live on my own

please turn over

You and your family

Some people say that you can tell what young people are likely to do with their lives by looking at what their families do. For example, they say that young people with parents who have good jobs find it easier to get good jobs themselves than people whose parents are unemployed.

When we ask about your mother/father- we mean whoever you think of as being your mother/father - this may be a step-parent, foster-parent, adoptive parent or your natural parent.

25a Has your mother had a paid job in the last 5 years? *(please tick one box)*
- (50) ☐ yes *(please answer question 25b)*
- ☐ no
- ☐ don't know/does not apply

25b What kind of paid work has your mother done?
(write in) ....(51-52)

26 Which of these best describe what your mother is doing at the moment?
(tick as many boxes as you need)
- (53) ☐ looking after the family
- (54) ☐ unemployed
- (55) ☐ working full-time in a paid job
- (56) ☐ studying
- (57) ☐ working part-time in a paid job
- (58) ☐ something else *(please write in)*...
- (59) ☐ don't know/does not apply

27a Has your father had a paid job in the last 5 years? *(please tick one box)*
- (60) ☐ yes *(please answer question 27b)*
- ☐ no
- ☐ don't know/does not apply'

27b What kind of paid work has your father done?
(write in)...(61-62)

28 Which of these best describe what your father is doing at the moment?
(tick as many boxes as you need)
- (63) ☐ looking after the family
- (64) ☐ unemployed
- (65) ☐ working full-time in a paid job
- (66) ☐ studying
- (67) ☐ working part-time in a paid job
- (68) ☐ something else *(please write in)*...
- (69) ☐ don't know/does not apply

page 7

Your choice...

In the last booklet we asked everybody to choose an important subject to include in this questionnaire. The most popular choices were racism, crime and the police. Therefore, the next few questions are on those subjects.

29 Here are some statements about crime, the police and the law.
Tick one box for each statement to show whether you agree or disagree:

	agree	neither	disagree
Judges and courts give fair and equal treatment to everyone in this country.	☐	☐	☐ (70)
If I witness a crime, I keep my mouth shut because I don't want to become involved	☐	☐	☐ (71)

30a During the past year have you ever been stopped or asked questions by the police about an offence which they thought had been committed?
(please tick one box)

(8) ☐ yes *(please answer questions 30b and 30c)*
☐ no *(please go to question 31)*

30b If yes, about how many times have you been stopped in the past year?
(write in) about .... times

30c On those occasions, were the police generally polite or impolite when they approached you?
(please tick one box)

(11) ☐ very polite
☐ fairly polite
☐ fairly impolite
☐ very impolite
☐ sometimes polite, sometimes impolite

please turn over

31 Here are some statements about race and the police. *Please tick one box for each statement to show how strongly you agree or disagree.*

	strongly agree	agree	not sure	disagree	strongly disagree	
People from Black and Asian origin can rely on the police to protect them from racial harassment	☐	☐	☐	☐	☐	(12)
Black and Asian people should organise self-defence groups to protect themselves from racial attacks	☐	☐	☐	☐	☐	(13)
The police harass young Black people more than young white people	☐	☐	☐	☐	☐	(14)
The police harass young Asian people more than young white people	☐	☐	☐	☐	☐	(15)

32 How would you describe yourself? *(please tick one box)*
(16) ☐ very prejudiced against people of other races
☐ a little prejudiced against people of other races
☐ not at all prejudiced against people of other races
☐ don't know.

33 Are you male or female? *(please tick one box)*
(17) ☐ male
☐ female

34 How would you describe your ethnic origin? *(please tick one box)*
(18) ☐ Black African
☐ Black Caribbean
☐ Black other *(write in)*...
☐ Bangladeshi
☐ Chinese
☐ Indian
☐ Pakistani
☐ White
☐ Other *(write in)*...

And finally...

3 5 Has anyone in your family ever taken a degree course at university or polytechnic? *(tick as many boxes as you need)*

yes: (19)☐ my mother
(20)☐ my father
(21)☐ older brothers or sisters

no: (22)☐

3 6 Looking back, do you think you made the right or wrong decision about what to do at the end of year 11? *(please tick one box)*

(23) ☐ right decision
☐ wrong decision
☐ not sure
☐ I don't feel I had any choice

3 7 In about a year's time you will be able to vote in local and national elections. Which party do you think you will vote for? *(please tick one box)*

(24) ☐ Conservative
☐ Labour
☐ Liberal Democrat
☐ other *(please write in)* ....
☐ not sure
☐ I'm not going to vote

If you have any comments on the Changing Lives research or if there is anything else at all you want to say, please use the space below. This is your last opportunity!

3 8 ....

....

....

....

.... (25-26)

please turn over

That is the end of the Changing Lives project. Thank you again for taking part. Please don't forget to put your booklet in the envelope and post it back to us today. It does not need a stamp.

In the future, we may want to do more research into the experiences and ideas of young people. If you think you might be interested in taking part in other studies, please fill in your name and address below. You are not committing yourself to anything by doing this and your details will not be given to any other person or organisation.

Name ....

Address ....

....

.... Post code ....

Phone number (daytime) ....

Phone number (evenings) ....

Now please put this booklet into the reply paid envelope provided and post it off to us straight away. It does not need a stamp.

THANKS AGAIN FOR YOUR HELP.

If you would like further information about the Changing Lives survey, please contact: Catherine Shaw, Policy Studies Institute, 100 Park Village East, London NW1 3SR.